WHY
BUSHWICK
BILL
MATTERS

Music
Matters

Evelyn McDonnell and Oliver Wang,

Series Editors

WHY BUSHWICK BILL MATTERS

Charles L. Hughes

UNIVERSITY OF TEXAS PRESS

AUSTIN

Requests for permission to reproduce material from this work should be sent to:
 Permissions
 University of Texas Press
 P.O. Box 7819
 Austin, TX 78713-7819
 utpress.utexas.edu/rp-form

♾ The paper used in this book meets the minimum requirements of
ANSI/NISO Z39.48-1992 (R1997) (Permanence of Paper).

Library of Congress Cataloging-in-Publication Data
Names: Hughes, Charles L., 1982– author.
Title: Why Bushwick Bill matters / Charles L. Hughes.
Other titles: Music matters.
Description: First edition. | Austin : University of Texas Press, 2021. |
Series: Music matters | Includes bibliographical references.
Identifiers:
 LCCN 2020051378
 ISBN 978-1-4773-2231-4 (paperback)
 ISBN 978-1-4773-2342-7 (library ebook
 ISBN 978-1-4773-2343-4 (ebook)
Subjects: LCSH: Bushwick Bill. | Bushwick Bill—Influence. | Bushwick Bill—Political
and social views. | Rap musicians—United States—Biography. | Dwarfs (Persons)—
United States—Biography. | Musicians with disabilities—United States—Biography.
Classification: LCC ML420.B8976 H85 2021 | DDC 782.421649092 [B]—dc23
LC record available at https://lccn.loc.gov/2020051378

doi:10.7560/322314

For Ari

CONTENTS

A NOTE ON TERMINOLOGY

The question of what to call members of a disabled community has long been crucial and complicated. The terms by which we're identified help us control our own identities, erase harmful slurs or stereotypes, and shape larger conversations about how we want outsiders to describe us. But this process can be thorny, especially given the lack of consensus on which terms are preferred and appropriate, as well as the shifting connotations of some terms once found either acceptable or problematic. I have experienced this throughout my life. I'm a short person who has been referred to by the range of names (both hurtful and well-intentioned) that have been assigned to folks like me, and so was Bushwick Bill. Before moving forward, I want to briefly address the approach I use here.

When discussing Bushwick Bill, I primarily use *short* or *short person*, which corresponds with how he most frequently described himself both on record and in interviews. I will also refer to myself with this language, as well as occasionally using the related term *short-statured*. And I will use *short* and *short-statured* more generally as descriptors when the individuals' self-identification is unclear. Bushwick Bill also referred to himself as a dwarf in several song lyrics and at least once in an interview. Many short people identify as dwarfs, and dwarfism remains an accepted description of a physiological condition.[1] But others prefer other terms or use *dwarf* only as a noun or adjective (for example, "dwarf person").[2] I will use the term primarily when it appears in sources and context, but also as a modifying adjective or when it is clear that the people I am discussing are using it to identify themselves.

The term *little person* is another alternative developed from within the community that has become common for both organizations and individuals. The Little People of America, the first and largest advocacy organization for people with dwarfism, uses it, as do prominent contemporary figures such as the writer and activist Rebecca Cokley. I have not found evidence of Bushwick Bill referring to himself as a little person, and I've resisted using it to describe myself. (I find it too reminiscent of cutesy and infantilizing terms that I've been called over the years. But that's just me.) I honor the term's use by those who identify as little people and will use it when describing them.

I recognize that this is not a perfect solution. I hope that I have avoided using terms in problematic or overcomplicated ways. Also, as everyone involved in these conversations reminds us, the best way to refer to a person is by their name, which I will do. I can only assure you that I've made my best effort.[3]

In addition, there are places in the book where I reference song lyrics and statements that include language that some readers may find offensive. These include not only the N-word but also other slurs and descriptions of violence, including sexual assault. I have kept this language to a minimum, but please be aware that it does appear in the text.

WHY
BUSHWICK
BILL
MATTERS

INTRODUCTION

In 1989 the Houston rap group the Geto Boys included a blistering track called "Size Ain't Shit" on their breakthrough album, *Grip It! On That Other Level.* The song paid profane tribute to the sexual prowess and overall toughness of group member Bushwick Bill and doesn't diverge much from the rest of their incendiary catalog, which rattled speakers and angered detractors for more than two decades. Only one thing makes it exceptional: "Size Ain't Shit" is a tribute to its performer's shortness. Over a clattering track, Bushwick Bill — born with dwarfism — unleashes a furious set of rhymes to discuss how, in the bedroom and elsewhere, "large things come in very small packages." Raw and rowdy, "Size Ain't Shit" became his anthem as he and the Geto Boys became famous — and infamous — across the world.

Born in Jamaica and raised in New York, Bushwick Bill (born Richard Shaw) played a crucial role in the Geto Boys as they became one of the most important hip-hop groups of all time. Exploding out of Houston in the late 1980s, the group released five albums and three singles that reached the Billboard Rap Top 10; three of those albums earned gold or platinum status, and two of the singles crossed over to the Pop Top 40. Their commercial success understates their impact, as Geto Boys records (particularly those made by the classic lineup of Scarface, Willie D, Bushwick Bill, and DJ Ready Red) became key to the early '90s rap renaissance. They were critical to the growth of Houston's prosperous rap scene and the broader emergence of "Dirty South" hip-hop as a creative and commercial force. The group remains influential for contemporary artists, from Megan Thee Stallion to Kendrick Lamar to Eminem.

At the same time, the Geto Boys became lightning rods in the culture wars of the 1990s. Like their contemporaries 2 Live Crew and N.W.A., the group attracted criticism throughout the decade from figures ranging from Republican presidential candidate Bob Dole to former New York City mayor Ed Koch to Dr. C. DeLores Tucker, all of whom condemned the group for its ultraviolent content and misogynist language. Conversely, the group was championed by those who defended rap — even the hardcore rhymes of the Geto Boys — as a necessary and legitimate expression of Black experiences in the late Reagan era. Both loved and hated, the Geto Boys embodied the tumultuous debates over pop music's social impact in the era of anti-rap crusades and emergent hip-hop politics.

Bushwick Bill was pivotal to the group's success and notoriety. Originally hired as a dancer and hype man for the group's live performances, he developed a singular voice within the Geto Boys and became what one writer called their "visual signature" thanks to his unique appearance.[1] His verses on hits such as "My Mind's Playing Tricks on Me" and "Damn It Feels Good To Be A Gangsta," as well as solo showcases such as "Chuckie" and "Size Ain't Shit," mixed profane blues humor, grotesque horror fantasies, and vulnerable reflections that both counteracted and complemented the group's outrageousness. Bill also contributed some of the group's most potent political critiques. On tracks such as "Fuck a War" and "Crooked Officer," he decries racism, hypocrisy, and injustice with a fire and detail that extended into public life, where he became the Geto Boys' primary spokesman in their period of greatest notoriety. As the ethnomusicologist Langston Collin Wilkins notes, Bill "was able to use [his] bone-chilling, sometimes emotionless yet captivating voice and delivery to detail the psychological struggles that come with living in an urban environment as an African-American."[2] This signature mix characterized Bill's contributions to the Geto Boys' albums and a solo career that stretched from 1992's *Little Big Man* (which produced the hit single "Ever So Clear") through 2009's gospel detour, *My Testimony of Redemption*. When Bill died in 2019 of pancreatic cancer, artists and fans saluted an artistic voice that was made even more singular by the body that produced it.

Bushwick Bill talked about shortness a lot on his records. He mixed "Size Ain't Shit" braggadocio with earnest accountings of how his height limited him as he walked (and swaggered) through a world built for taller folks. He condemned the physical barriers and social stigmas of an ableist world, which he connected to larger critiques of racism, poverty, and hypocrisy. He insisted that his small stature only accentuated his status as a badass who could handle any full-sized joker who might underestimate him, whether those aggressors originated on the corner or in the White House. And he talked about sex. He presented himself as "the little motherfucker with the big dick swingin'" whose abilities pleased all the women, and he sometimes rapped about sexual violence in verses that were framed as fictional but were part of his larger, unseemly use of misogynist and queerphobic language. Bushwick Bill, the "little big man," performed the exaggerated masculinity that was common in gangsta rap through a body type often coded as sexually unappealing or nonfunctional.

Bushwick Bill thus focused pop music's attention on physical disability and flipped the script on the able-bodied gawk that the pioneering theorist Rosemarie Garland-Thomson calls "the stare." "Perhaps the most spectacular form of visual novelty that can prompt stares are breaches of the common human scale and shape," Garland-Thomson observes, noting that dwarfs provoke particularly intense curiosity as "figures of contradiction to the eye of an ordinary starer."[3] Beyond questions over how they perform everyday activities, from shopping to sex, short people also embody "shared stories" ranging "from sentimental and cute to grotesque and vengeful."[4]

Bushwick Bill offered a furious remix of these narratives. His declarations of full, even excessive masculinity refuted associations of dwarfs with cuteness or immaturity, from the playful Munchkins to the tragic Tiny Tim. At the same time, he performed a trickster re-appropriation of perceptions of dwarfs as dangerous. "Bodies that are disabled can also seem dangerous because they are perceived as out of control," Garland-Thomson notes, both because "they violate physical norms" and because "they threaten to disrupt the ritualized behavior upon which social relations turn."[5] Bushwick Bill's refusal to play by these rules earned him both acclaim and condemnation. In the early '90s, he even adopted an alter ego who personified these dynamics: Chuckie, modeled after the evil doll of the *Child's Play* movies.

Bushwick Bill also used Chuckie to discuss mental health, which became a signature feature of his work, especially following the 1991 incident in which he shot himself in the eye during a failed suicide attempt (memorialized on the infamous cover of the Geto Boys' album *We Can't Be Stopped*). Bill recorded several songs that examine the depression, paranoia, and addiction that he had experienced throughout his life. Mental illness, along with his lost eye, became additional markers of difference that Bill discussed in complex, sometimes painful ways, from "Ever So Clear" through his final releases. He linked these conditions to his size, exploring the real links between mental health and ableist/racist oppression while refuting unfair assumptions about the relationship between his stature and his psychology.

By foregrounding disability in these ways, Bushwick Bill is unique in the history of popular music. He's the only performer with dwarfism to achieve mainstream pop fame, and one of the few musicians with a noticeable physical disability to address it in such a direct and sustained manner. Bolstered by rap's paradoxical balance of realness and fantasy, Bill performed what George McKay calls "a sign of dissension and critique . . . as the monstrous, deviant, or different stigmatized identity is claimed, staged, sounded and flaunted."[6] From "Size Ain't Shit" forward, Bushwick Bill insisted that listeners confront a short-statured person who was funny, fierce, thoughtful, and — sometimes — totally fucked up.

Although he's a singular figure, Bushwick Bill also reflects larger histories. Beyond his importance to the rap wars of the Reagan and Clinton years, which symbolized longstanding tensions associated with Black culture and its relationship to white America, Bushwick Bill reflected and refracted the longer history of disability politics and culture. He engaged the ambivalent legacies of nineteenth-century freak shows, which offered an early opportunity for disabled performers to achieve popularity but also ensured, as Joseph Straus notes, that "the disabled performer has a dual task: to perform music and to perform disability" for audiences who do not share their difference.[7]

Bill also emerged at the same time as the pivotal Americans with Disabilities Act, and he both symbolized the moment's new opportunities and challenged mainstream representations of disabled people. Uncontained and uncontrolled, Bushwick Bill reflected radical traditions in disability activism and presaged a new generation that is benefiting from the breakthroughs of earlier eras while demanding a new form of address.

I'm one of that generation. Living as a short-statured person, I confront a world that wasn't built for me and is continually disrupted by my presence. I've been perceived as childlike and seen my body considered a problem. And I've experienced the fact that whether or not we work as performers, those of us who are perceived as disabled live our lives on stage. No matter who we are or where we go, we are always the "human exhibits" of the freak shows, forced to consider how what Garland-Thomson calls our "extraordinary bodies" might be interpreted (and stared at) by normal folks. Bushwick Bill has given me a booming soundtrack for my attempts to navigate that world and survive that hypervisibility. In his defiance and joy, Bushwick Bill remains a role model for me in how to live as a short person in all its messy complexity. So, although what follows is not a memoir, I hope to honor how Bushwick Bill has improved my life as I consider his broader impact on the world.

I'm aware of some pitfalls. For one, I'm white, which

renders my experience very different from Bushwick Bill's and means that my fandom risks its own kind of racial exoticism. My admiration for him can't help but reflect a bit of Eric Lott's minstrel-esque "love and theft," as well as concerns about why white people love gangsta rap.[8] Also, there were moments in Bushwick Bill's public life that are troubling, and I'm going to address them. And I'll try to avoid overcorrecting into the ableist or racist zone by suggesting that his work was solely an expression of his lived experience. As Langston Collin Wilkins notes, Bill's songs "were intensely personal, and he expressed them through . . . creative means" by crafting fictional versions of deeper truths.[9] "You pick your own lane and create your own character," he reminded us, and Richard Shaw developed his character, Bushwick Bill, over three decades.[10]

Finally, I'll try to heed Rosemarie Garland-Thomson's advice to not reduce the work of a disabled artist to a "single stigmatic trait," even if the goal is to celebrate what was previously stigmatized.[11] Bushwick Bill's talents distinguish him both alongside and outside of his physical difference, and while his music was shaped by his physicality, it was far from the only thing he rapped about or cared about. Even as he expressed disabled experiences amidst historical stereotypes and contemporary limitations, he also insisted that we not reduce his experiences by focusing on him only as a physical oddity. "Being short, I believe people looked and stared at me my whole life before I ever got on stage and rapped," he recalled in 2015. "Now it's not 'look at the short guy,' it's 'It's Bushwick Bill!'"[12]

"Most people have forgotten how dope Bushwick was," the music critic Shea Serrano wrote in 2009. "Don't."[13] What follows is my attempt to show just how much is there to remember.

HOW LITTLE BILLY BECAME BUSHWICK BILL

Everybody in the Houston club noticed the breakdancer known as Little Billy. "You know, you in the club, you not used to something that low," remembered DJ Ready Red, the man spinning the records. "I was like 'Aw, it's this cat right here.'"[1] Brad Jordan, a rapper who later performed as Scarface, saw Little Billy flirting with a woman at the bar.[2] And James Prince, an aspiring entrepreneur, remembered the man he called the "dwarf who I met in the club" when he put together a group that he hoped would capture the excitement of Houston's burgeoning rap scene. Prince called that group the Ghetto Boys.[3]

Bill's involvement with the group (who later changed the spelling to "Geto Boys") stretches from its inception to its conclusion; he's the only member who appeared on both their first and last albums. He was initially hired to be a dancer in the group's live performances, chosen both for his breakdancing skills — which gave the group an authentic connection to hip-hop's New York roots — and for his size, which gave them a unique look that they hoped would turn heads. But even before he started rapping, Bill influenced the direction of the group as they established a creative and commercial foothold. And as the Geto Boys took shape, Little Billy became Bushwick Bill.

Richard Shaw's journey to Houston mirrored that of the music he made his life's work. He was born in Kingston, Jamaica, in 1966 and moved with his family (including eight siblings) to New York in 1973. "He came from a hardworking family where everybody doin' something," his son recalled later.[4] Settling in the Bushwick neighborhood of Brooklyn, Shaw's father worked as a Merchant Marine, and his mother as a hotel maid.

The Shaws arrived as part of a larger migration of Jamaicans to the United States. In the aftermath of the 1965 Hart-Celler Immigration and Naturalization Act, which ended previous racialized quotas and installed a proportional immigration system, an influx of people from the Caribbean (along with counterparts from Africa, Asia, and Latin America) arrived in the United States. Most of them settled in urban areas, including New York. They lived primarily in historically Black and Brown communities, as well as neighborhoods that had suffered structural abandonment in the years of de-industrialization and "white flight." As Shaw grew up, he witnessed that process in Bushwick.

Rap arrived in New York the same year, and via the same route, as the Shaw family. In 1973, in the South Bronx, a Jamaican immigrant named DJ Kool Herc hosted a dance party that many consider the origin point for hip-hop culture.[5] Herc modeled his music on the mobile sound systems that DJs drove around Kingston: two turntables, where they mixed the pulsing beats of local dub and reggae hits with the funky sounds of American R&B and disco, over which the DJs shouted semi-improvised rhymes designed to promote themselves, excite the dancers, and call together the community. The nascent sounds of rap music soon provided a soundtrack for Black and Brown communities (both preexisting and newly arrived) in the Big Apple, from private parties to public parks. DJ Kool Herc and other hip-hop pioneers developed a musical culture that symbolized the trans-Atlantic collisions and connections that re-created the South Bronx and other parts of the city, including Bushwick.

From its inception, hip-hop culture involved not just a musical revolution but also accompanying movements in dance and visual art. Breakdancing and graffiti developed alongside rap as crucial components of New York's hip-hop scene, and it was these forms that gave Shaw his first direct entry into the culture as a participant. They provided what Maco Faniel has described as "solace and excitement," an outlet for his skills and a way to counteract the marginalization he experienced because of his size.[6] In a duality recognizable to many disabled people, Shaw had developed a standoffish personality meant to ward off potential threats, along with an extroverted side that used humor and talent to ingratiate himself with others.[7] He found a home for those talents, and perhaps that swagger, in graffiti and breakdancing in his teenage years.[8] He became proficient enough to join a competitive break-dance crew, and he painted under the name INFANT, an evocative name given his shortness.[9] According to his son, Shaw even led his own graffiti crew, the Bushwick Posse.[10] These crews and collectives were crucial to hip-hop's early days. Beyond propelling the growth of the culture, they provided a space for nonviolent competition and support-ive community in a period of structural abandonment. For Shaw, whose size rendered him different from an early age, his presence, and even leadership, within hip-hop's flour-ishing networks gave him a crucial opportunity to belong.[11]

Years before he arrived in Houston, and long before he became a Geto Boy, Shaw was incorporating rap's global flows and local characteristics at rap's ground zero. Making the connections even more direct, his sister married a Jamaican-born DJ, and in the mid-1980s the couple moved to Houston. Shaw, meanwhile, took a different path. Long interested in spirituality, and a skilled orator, he left New York to attend Bible college in Minnesota. He imagined that this education would provide the first step in his planned career as minister and missionary. After graduating, before he was scheduled to leave for a mission trip to India, he came to Houston to visit his sister and brother-in-law.

By moving to Houston, Shaw's family took part in an-other crucial demographic shift that proved critical to the history of hip-hop. The Shaws were part of an early wave in the "reverse" Great Migration, which brought Black folks back to the South (or to the South for the first time) in the final decades of the twentieth century. This trend was critical to the growth of Southern hip-hop, both by creating cross-regional musical links between North and South, and by spurring the growth of southern record companies and other infrastructure to produce and market the music. Houston was an early site for both the migration and the records that emerged from it. And just like his move to New York as a kid, Shaw was there from the beginning.

He was soon spotted on the dance floor at local clubs. A talented breaker, an authentic New Yorker, and a dwarf at that, Shaw (by then known as Little Billy) was noticed at clubs like the Rhinestone Wrangler, one of the pivotal locations for the development of Houston's rap scene. "The first time I had an opportunity to lay eyes on him, he was dancing," James Prince remembered. "The energy that he was putting in that dance was amazing."[12] DJ Ready Red, then spinning at the Rhinestone Wrangler, was particularly impressed. "Bill's a b-boy," he recalled, using the descriptor given to male breakers. "I was a breakdance DJ, so I'd put the breaks on" (referring to the brief rhythmic sections from disco and funk tracks that DJs would loop and mix for the dancers), "and Bill could just cut it up, man."[13] Ready Red (born Collins Leysath) was a northerner himself, having moved from New Jersey, so he recognized the legitimacy of Little Billy's moves. Shaw's Houston sojourn was supposed to be temporary, but after meeting Ready Red and others, he changed his plans. Instead of going to India "to build irrigation systems, schools and indoor plumbing," he joined a new crew, a group of artists and entrepreneurs working to put Houston on the map for rap music.[14]

The Geto Boys would get credit for making Houston a rap city, but the roots of the scene were established long before the group's formation. "In the mid-1980s," Maco Faniel recalled, "Houston was a major participant in hip-hop culture prior to showcasing its own artists and styles." This was thanks to the proliferation of rap-focused nightclubs such as the Rhinestone Wrangler, as well as record stores and radio shows. DJ Ready Red remembered that "there was always DJs in a warehouse that you go to, and they always had people on the mic that was good. They were actually doin' hip-hop but they didn't know that was the term for it. Houston always had its place with the rap."[15]

The growth of H-Town hip-hop was the latest chapter in Houston's storied history of musical innovation. With labels, venues, and vibrant professional networks, the city had already left a significant mark on jazz, blues, soul, and other genres. As Tyina L. Steptoe notes, the city's unique music reflected its identity as a social and cultural crossroads for Black, Brown, and white communities from Texas, Louisiana, Mexico, and elsewhere.[16] This mix, which Steptoe calls Houston's "multi-racial/multi-ethnic metropolis," created distinctive artists, including Lightnin' Hopkins, Archie Bell and the Drells, and later Beyonce and Solange Knowles.[17] Houston rap entered this continuum. As Scarface remembered, "We get all sorts of people passing through Houston, from all sorts of places, and they always bring their influences and then we mix that with what we've always had going on and that's where the city's culture comes from." By mixing East Coasters with members from different neighborhoods in Houston, "The Geto Boys were a great example of that."[18]

The music wasn't the only similarity between Houston and New York. Although the bustling economy of the Sun Belt in the 1970s had spurred the city's growth, by the mid-1980s that prosperity had both waned and been centralized in wealthier, whiter neighborhoods. Maco Faniel has pointed out that "Houston also began to experience mass suburbanization," which, when "coupled with high unemployment, low-wage jobs and deteriorating public schools, made working-class black neighborhoods invisible and susceptible to increased criminal activity, surveillance and nihilism."[19] The economic and social conditions that precipitated the rise of hip-hop in the South Bronx were paralleled in several places in and around Houston.

Perhaps the most notoriously disadvantaged neighborhood was Fifth Ward, which had been a center of historic Black accomplishment. "African Americans in Houston championed the maintenance and protection of black communities as an issue of race pride," Tyina Steptoe notes, "and they used neighborhoods like Fifth Ward as buffers against white supremacy."[20] But over the century, the neighborhood (also known as the Bloody Nickel due to its crime rate) became a vivid demonstration of the abandonment facing Black Houstonians. James Prince recognized that these conditions created particularly fertile ground for a new rap scene. "The overall feeling throughout Houston was one of abundance," he observed. "But that feeling of excess, of financial possibilities, of hope, somehow skipped over the Fifth Ward."[21]

Prince hoped to leverage both creativity and challenge through a new label, Rap-a-Lot Records. "When we were coming up," remembered Scarface, "we were always getting music from other cities, however we could," but Rap-a-Lot would provide an outlet for distinctively local sounds.[22] Prince modeled the label, formed in 1987, after successful New York imprints like Def Jam, which was then at the height of its powers with Run-DMC, the Beastie Boys, and other groups who combined booming tracks with quick interplay between emcees. In the early days, Prince even opened a Rap-a-Lot office in Manhattan to be closer to the action, a move that symbolized his awareness of New York's musical and commercial centrality in the hip-hop world.

But Prince also recognized the need to keep Rap-a-Lot distinctly Houston. An early part of the larger growth of southern rap during the 1980s, Rap-a-Lot aimed to challenge New York's hegemony by consolidating, celebrating, and capitalizing on the talent pool already rocking the mic in clubs throughout the city. To do this, Prince hired DJ Ready Red as in-house producer, and he recalled that "Red worked in that room day and night, making beats, coming up with song concepts and defining our sound."[23] Prince focused particular attention on creating the Ghetto Boys, a group of rappers that he believed would be the label's premiere artists.

Like that of his label, Prince's vision for the Ghetto Boys was modeled on the New York–based groups that defined the genre. "Crews, from like the original hip-hop," remembered DJ Ready Red, "those guys were all together before they even thought of makin' records."[24] Pulling together three well-known Houston emcees, Prince released one single, the Run-DMC homage "Car Freak," but it attracted limited attention. Two of the emcees departed, and Prince reassembled the group around Sire Jukebox (who remained from the first group), Johnny C (a new rapper), and DJ Ready Red. To round out the lineup, he hired Richard Shaw (who had changed his stage name from Little Billy to the neighborhood-repping Bushwick Bill) to spice up the group's live performances with his breakdancing and lend the group additional New York authenticity.[25] Shaw remembered that when he inquired about his role in the group, Prince told him that his dance moves — "lockin', poppin', whatever it is you're doing" — would be a perfect addition. "I've seen all this in movies but we need that for the image of the group."[26]

Despite his importance to their live shows, Bushwick Bill was almost entirely absent from the Ghetto Boys' 1988 debut, *Making Trouble*. He appears on the album cover but doesn't rap on the record; Johnny C and Sire Jukebox did the lion's share of the rhyming, and even DJ Ready Red got a showcase number. Bill's absence from its contents is not the only way that *Making Trouble* remains an outlier in the Geto Boys' discography. Its personnel, sound, and iconography bear little resemblance to the recordings that made them famous. "We were tryin' to be commercial," DJ Ready Red admitted. "We did what we heard [Run-DMC] doin', what we heard the Fat Boys doin'. We was tryin' to be commercial, acceptable."[27]

Run-DMC remained the album's most obvious touchstone. The spare tracks and measured rhymes are highly reminiscent of their signature musical style, and the cover image — which finds the Ghetto Boys clad in black leather jackets, hats, and gold chains — directly mimicked the group's look. Songs on *Making Trouble* aped the group's well-known tracks: the Ghetto Boys copped Run-DMC's hit "Rock Box" in the thump of the Queen-sampling "Geto Boys Will Rock You," and the message song "Why Do We Live This Way?" quotes lines from Run-DMC's thematically similar "It's Like That." One track, "One Time (Freestyle)," even features Jukebox saying that the group represents "Fifth Ward not Hollis, Queens," referencing Run-DMC's oft-mentioned home turf in an early example of H-Town pride.

As much as it reflected New York influence, *Making Trouble* also signaled the rise of a different strain of rap then emerging on the West Coast. "If you compare the *Making Trouble* album to the first N.W.A. album," Ready Red told

Lance Scott Walker, "you'll see [they are very] similar concept-wise."[28] The influence of N.W.A.'s debut, *Straight Outta Compton*, on the Geto Boys and hip-hop in general is hard to overstate. Released in 1988, it signaled the national emergence of gangsta rap, a Los Angeles–based style that mixed exaggerated narratives of crime and excess with unvarnished descriptions of police misconduct, poverty, and other injustices faced by Black communities in the late Reagan era.[29]

This profane and provocative blend, sometimes called "reality rap" to reflect its brutal lyrics, also signaled a crucial regional shift.[30] *Straight Outta Compton* became the first hit rap album produced outside of New York, suggesting a template for local scenes that diverged from the Big Apple model. The Geto Boys, Rap-a-Lot, and Houston would be among the first to follow in N.W.A.'s footsteps. Gangsta played a particularly significant role in the Houston sound that emerged alongside the linked but distinct hip-hop scenes throughout the South. But other than the cold-blooded crime spree track "Assassins," rapped by Johnny C., *Making Trouble* only hinted at what was to come.

Similarly, Bushwick Bill's sole appearance on *Making Trouble* portended his future role. At the end of the album, on the spoken-word track "The Problem," Bill shows up to talk about his size. "The Problem" features a conversation between the group's members discussing various problems they've faced and what they predict will happen going forward. When considering what his problem might be, Bill asks, "Is it because I'm too short to take shorts?," referencing a slang abbreviation for "shortcuts."[31] Later, bored by what the others are saying, he says, "I'm too short for a long conversation." What might seem like a throwaway also establishes a template; going forward, Bill would use his size to offer a unique and disruptive perspective. Like *Making Trouble* as a whole, Bill's appearance points a way forward even as it reveals the album's limitations.

Released on Rap-a-Lot Records in 1988, *Making Trouble* sold well regionally but made little national impact. "Before that album, nobody was talking about the South," James Prince claims. "That release gave my city hope that more was on the way."[32] Its limited success, combined with the post-N.W.A. growth of gangsta as a commercial force, convinced Prince and DJ Ready Red to reimagine the group as more Houston and more harrowing. They sought to amplify local connections, especially to Fifth Ward, and they planned to build on "Assassins" by making the lyrical content more extreme. As Ready Red recalled, they hoped to exceed the violence of N.W.A. and other gangstas by taking their lyrics further than anyone else. "We're talkin' about drug dealin', slayin', havin' sex with headless corpses and all this other crazy stuff, man."[33]

As part of this process, Sire Jukebox and Johnny C departed. "It was always going to be Geto Boys," DJ Ready Red claimed, "just like there was numerous Temptations changes and New Editions lineups and all that. That's just how it happens sometimes."[34] Their replacements earned their spots due to their closeness to the group's new approach. Willie D (born William Dennis) was the only member to have lived in Fifth Ward, offering neighborhood credibility while also contributing a fierce lyrical and vocal style that expanded and sharpened their palette. "I brought social and political awareness, but I was also the straight-up rebel," Willie D remembered. "I just didn't give a fuck about nothin'!"[35] To accompany him, they hired Brad Jordan, who had performed and recorded as Akshen but was renamed Scarface. Jordan's lyrics blended graphic extremes with brooding reflections, delivered in a thunderous voice that amplified his meditations and anchored even his wildest fantasies. One of those compositions, the song "Scarface," reflects what Jordan called "all of the shit we'd been doing in the streets" and references a cinematic touchstone favored by his bandmates even before he joined.[36]

According to Maco Faniel, "[DJ Ready] Red recalled that while working on [*Making Trouble*], he and Little Billy were watching *Scarface* and that when they heard Pacino's famous sound bites, they both had an 'aha' moment."[37] Ready Red placed samples from the Brian de Palma film throughout *Making Trouble*, most prominently on "Balls and My Word," and when Jordan was hired, the two remaining group members saw an opportunity to solidify their relationship to the movie by linking the newest member to Pacino's antihero.[38] Not only did it fit his persona and offer a basis for additional tracks featuring the character, but DJ Ready Red recognized a happy coincidence within the group's personnel. "'I started putting together these Scarface concepts," he told Roni Sarig, "'Say hello to my little friend' and all that stuff. Bill became the 'little friend,' so everything started working out for us.'"[39]

Bushwick Bill survived the roster shake-up, but the "little friend" remained a mostly silent hype man whose role in the Geto Boys as an onstage dancer was to lend the group both authenticity and novelty. This mixture of skills and spectacle, briefly glimpsed on *Making Trouble*, led to his induction as a full group member. One night in the studio, Willie D heard him rapping along to "Rebel Without a Pause" by the New York–based group Public Enemy. Recently released on their 1988 breakout album, *It Takes a Nation of Millions to Hold Us Back*, the song was an appropriate choice.

Although the group's influence is not as obvious as N.W.A.'s, Public Enemy was another important touchstone for the Geto Boys. Debuting in 1987, the group mixed dense, politicized rhymes—delivered primarily by leader Chuck D, but also by their crucial second emcee, Flavor Flav—with multilayered, sample-heavy tracks created by their producers, the Bomb Squad. The pairing of militant lyrics with clattering productions made Public Enemy a key East Coast complement and counterpoint to the West Coast's gangsta blast. Sitting in the literal and figurative middle ground, the Geto Boys incorporated the sonic and thematic lessons of both as they constructed their "third coast" synthesis. After invoking Run-DMC on *Making Trouble*, their second album would place them in conversation with both N.W.A. and Public Enemy, and the regional innovations they symbolized, by asserting a uniquely Houston identity. And this time, Bushwick Bill's voice would be in the mix.

When Willie D heard Bushwick Bill rhyming "Rebel Without a Pause," both men recognized an opportunity. "I looked at him and a light just went off in my head," Willie D remembered. "That would be some trip shit to see a midget rap."[40] James Prince "was apprehensive at first," Willie D claimed, and he even remembers some people laughing at the idea,[41] but Willie was convinced. "I said, 'Let me write him a rap, and if he can do the rap let him be in the group.'" After they spoke, and after Willie "asked [Bill] some personal things about himself," they emerged with the lyrics for "Size Ain't Shit."[42] It's not clear how much of the song was a stylized transcription of Bill's thoughts and how much was Willie D's invention, but Bushwick Bill seized the opportunity. "He didn't wanna be a gimmick," group associate Raheem recalled, "so they said, 'Aight, we'll have somebody write something for you, and you'll be in the group, you'll be a rapper.'"[43] "Size Ain't Shit" became an anthem for Bushwick Bill and a key track on the Geto Boys' breakthrough next album, 1989's *Grip It! On That Other Level*.

Even before its release, the journey to "Size Ain't Shit" captured Richard Shaw's story in vivid microcosm. He was a Jamaican-born, New York-raised performer who earned his place in Houston's first major hip-hop group because of his breakdancing skills and unique physicality. In both cities he used rap to resist his outsider status by developing talents that gave him at least some opportunity to join the party. He contributed to the Geto Boys' direction and distinguished them onstage as they built and refined their group identity. And he became a full-fledged member both because of his ability to perform the furious rhymes of New York's latest rap kings and because of the "trip shit" of seeing "a midget rap."

The road from Little Billy to "Size Ain't Shit" traced an additional history. As a prominent disabled performer whose shortness became central to his work, Bushwick Bill reflected and remixed a longer, more ambivalent tradition. When he stepped up to the mic, Bill didn't just add a crucial new voice to the rap conversation. He bum-rushed the freak show.

BUM-RUSH THE FREAK SHOW

Bushwick Bill's breakthrough sprang from a simple premise: Willie D thought it would be "some trip shit" to see a "midget rap." And the song "Size Ain't Shit" certainly was unprecedented, both for its content and for the artist who rapped it. But Willie D's initial impulse to exploit the surprise and spectacle of seeing a short person rap revealed the song's place within a longer history. By launching Bushwick Bill's career, "Size Ain't Shit" offered a new chapter in the narrow and complicated space for people with dwarfism as well as other disabled performers in pop music.

Most specifically, Bushwick Bill remixed the legacies of freak shows in the United States. Hugely popular in the nineteenth century, freak shows — the display of human "oddities" in theatrical settings that ranged from proscenium stages to roadside carnivals — offered both a dehumanizing spectacle and a surprising entry point for disabled performers. Additionally, freak shows helped construct ideas of disability and race that connected to broader shifts in American politics and culture. Even after they declined in popularity in the twentieth century, the ideological and practical consequences of the freak shows structured the careers of disabled musicians and other entertainers. As the musicologist Joseph Straus notes, "If musical performers have extraordinary, prodigious, even monstrous bodies, then musical performances have an aspect of a freak show."[1] Bushwick Bill both resisted and embodied this complex dynamic.

Short people have been the subject of fascination for much of recorded human history. Betty Adelson notes that in earlier centuries short people held "ambivalent" status as both curiosity and outcast, variously marginalized, displayed, and thought to possess special or even dangerous powers because of their physical difference. This mixture of fear and awe led to, among other things, the use of court dwarfs, who stood next to the throne as markers of royal wealth and power in societies from China to Great Britain.[2] As the practice waned through the 1600s, many short-statured people, whose other career opportunities remained significantly limited, pivoted from one form of display to another. Now promoting themselves, they launched careers as self-exhibitors who entertained audiences through their physical novelty and, whenever possible, "some ostensible talent, enabling them to believe that the audience valued them for their stellar performances."[3] In fairs, circuses, and theatres, dwarfs joined other unusual people in displaying themselves as curiosities, thus earning a consistent if limited role as a source of delight for regular-sized audiences.

It makes sense, then, that short people would be a staple of the freak shows that emerged in the United States in the 1800s. These shows were the latest version of a longer history of gawking curiosity, but they also evinced a specific set of historical circumstances. They not only reflected the growth of popular culture and national media but also enacted what Rosemarie Garland-Thomson calls a "range of anxieties accompanying the social disorder in the United States" in the tumultuous period surrounding the Civil War.[4] Fittingly, the most significant anxiety concerned the question of who and what should be considered American.

Freak shows delineated physical and social boundaries between race, gender, and nationality. Garland-Thomson writes that audiences "needed to constantly reaffirm the difference between 'them' and 'us' at a time when immigration, emancipation of the slaves, and female suffrage confounded previously reliable physical indices of status and privilege."[5] The freak shows were a way to safely view tantalizing figures in an environment that wouldn't challenge the audience members' power or perceived inclusion in the safe "us" category. In this way, Thomson suggests, freak shows "symbolically contained the potential threat" by "exoticizing and trivializing bodies that were physically nonconformist."[6]

Within the many human exhibits on display, Black bodies played a particularly resonant role. Their race, combined with physical difference, contrasted with the reinforcement of whiteness as the biological, cultural, and political standard.[7] This impulse grew from the longstanding fascination of whites with commodification of Blackness, which extended back into European contact with Africans and then structured the system of American slavery, where disabled slaves were considered both less valuable and potentially less controllable.[8] "Concepts of race and disability were mutually constituted in nineteenth-century discourses," Dea H. Boster notes, with race and social status each becoming "a signifying marker in definitions of abnormal bodies."[9] The freak shows put these markers under the spotlight, offering a place of amusing catharsis for audiences who used freaky physicality to assure themselves of their own normality in the body politic.

No one was better at this than P. T. Barnum. The 1840 opening of Barnum's evocatively named American Theatre is often pegged as the beginning of modern freak spectacle, and the growth of his empire had a huge influence on the development of US popular culture, from circuses to vaudeville and beyond. Barnum's exhibits were vast and varied, but Bushwick Bill's historical predecessors played key roles in cementing Barnum's success.

"Dwarfs were Barnum's first successful human exhibits," writes David Gerber, "and they were to remain thereafter a staple item of all large freak shows."[10] The first of them was General Tom Thumb, a white man whose story reflects both the possibility and peril of the Barnum model as a profession for dwarf performers and others. Born Charles Stratton, Tom Thumb's military outfit and grand entrances delighted audiences who cheered and snickered at the juxtaposition between the big pageantry and the little man. His success with the Barnum crowds made him a breakout star; he later toured as both a solo act and with his wife Lavinia Warren, also short-statured, and their troupe of "Lilliputian" performers, one of several such outfits that toured the United States in this period. Tom Thumb's performances included impressions, dancing, and songs, reflecting both his facility with the range of talents required for nineteenth-century entertainers and the unique reactions produced when a short man displayed them. After he married Warren, his romantic life became a part of the show as source of marvel and mockery. "There was apt to be a straight man" in the performances, Betty Adelson notes, "drawing Thumb out about his success with the ladies."[11]

While Tom Thumb and Warren were his most famous "little" attractions, Barnum also presented African pygmies as examples of racial difference, curious physiognomy, and non-Western exoticism. This was part of Barnum's larger use of confined exhibits of Black people to affirm white power in a political environment where newly mobile Blacks were asserting their right to be considered full citizens. In 1836, Barnum launched his career with the touring exhibition of Joice Heth, the supposedly 161-year-old nursemaid of George Washington. "This black, disabled woman commodified as a freakish amusement testifies to America's need to ratify a dominant, normative identity by ritually displaying in public those perceived as the embodiment of what collective America took itself *not* to be," Garland-Thomson concludes.[12] (After Heth died, Barnum sold tickets to her autopsy.) Even more unsettling, Barnum later presented William Henry Johnson, a disabled Black man, under the banner of "What Is It?," encouraging audiences to determine if he was man, monkey, or some strange hybrid.[13]

Just as with the contemporaneous growth of blackface minstrelsy, the Black and disabled people whom Barnum and others presented as freaks tapped into white people's complex feelings about Blackness. African pygmies, for example, symbolized primitivism and affirmed the superiority of American civilization, but they also suggested a return to the supposed naturalness and simplicity of premodern life. Similarly, Benjamin Reiss suggests that Barnum's exhibition of Joice Heth both "exaggerated stereotypical attributes of blacks" and fed white nostalgia for Black servants and the Washingtonian era, by then a comforting counterpoint to the fractures of pre–Civil War America.[14] Bushwick Bill updated these dynamics for the late twentieth century, with his confrontational style and unique physicality symbolizing both the appeal and potential danger of rap culture in an era of reactionary conservatism.

Bushwick Bill also remixed the way that show business, even freak shows, offered opportunities for disabled people who had limited opportunities in other kinds of work. Promoters like Barnum wanted to assure their audiences that they were presenting legitimate (rather than fake) physical curiosities, so freak performers capitalized on their difference by assuring audiences that there was no one else like them. For them, like the self-exhibitors before them, the combination of physical difference and noteworthy talent made them more astonishing and, crucially, more marketable. As freak shows faded, in part because of the increasing perception that non-normative bodies were ugly afflictions that should be shielded from public view, many disabled musicians still engaged in this language to promote themselves to gawking audiences.

Generally speaking, the narratives surrounding disabled musicians fall into two connected categories. The first, as articulated by Joseph Straus, is to demean the music because of "the stigmatized quality of the body that produced it," which renders the music itself "deformed or defective." The second, what Straus calls "the narrative of overcoming," is meant to inspire audiences by demonstrating how the disabled musicians' accomplishments show their "elimination" or "normalization" of disability "in the course of a narrative trajectory toward normal selfhood."[15] All disabled people must navigate these twinned narratives in some fashion, and musicians offer various responses to this conundrum.

The situation for disabled Black performers was additionally complex, as evidenced by the experience of Tom Wiggins, who became a national sensation as the piano-playing attraction Blind Tom in the late 1800s. Both blind and what today would likely be diagnosed as autistic, Wiggins's unusual and compelling performances reconfirmed Black inferiority for white spectators even as they tapped into post-freak astonishment. As Terry Rowden explains, "He functioned as a living representation of the complexities of nineteenth-century America's cultural and political engagement with issues of racial and physical difference."[16] This white adulation drew criticism from some Black observers, who suggested that Blind Tom's fame confirmed white stereotypes and thus hindered the cause of racial advancement. As Rowden notes,

> In the immediate aftermath of the Civil War the self-consciously normalized image of black folk culture, represented by groups like the Fisk Jubilee Singers, was emerging as a challenge to the minstrel show stereotyping of blacks as buffoons and miscreants and the freak show presentation of all nonwhites as aberrant and socially unassimilable demi-humans who either came from or belonged somewhere else.[17]

Bushwick Bill faced a similar dynamic in the rap years. Like Blind Tom, Bill found, as Joseph Straus suggests, "his disabilities and his race [were] intertwined as aspects of his defective 'otherness'" for white audiences, and he would also face criticism as a debased confirmation of white distortions.[18]

The career of Blind Tom illustrated that disabled Black

musicians exist in the public imagination through a double-bound linkage of race and physical difference, whether as a defect or, increasingly, a symbol of perseverance. This tension is particularly evident in the numerous blues, gospel, jazz, and R&B artists who were defined by their blindness, which was used to promote them. Even transformative figures such as Ray Charles and Stevie Wonder embodied this narrative, marketed as savants in possession of what Wonder called "innervisions" that rendered their earthly blindness either moot or inspiring.[19] Later in his career, when Bushwick Bill became blind in one eye, he engaged this language. As he rapped on his solo hit "Ever So Clear," "It's fucked up I had to lose an eye to see things clearly."

The scarcity of performers with dwarfism precludes a similar tradition related to shortness. Short people of any race have been very rare in mainstream pop, although some prominent artists — including white country singer Little Jimmy Dickens and Black jazz-pop crooner Little Jimmy Scott — were noticeably smaller than average and incorporated their stature into songs, performances, and self-promotion. The appellation "Little" (and, in the hip-hop era, "Lil") remains common in describing artists of small size, but also of younger age and sometimes ambiguous gender performance. Many of the "little" musicians — including Dickens, Scott, and other performers, from gender-fucking Little Richard to R&B dynamo Little Esther Phillips to child lothario Lil Bow Wow — performed romantic material that made their perceived immaturity or distance from normative masculinity into both text and subtext for discussions of love and sex.

Sex is a troubled subject for disabled musicians, especially those whose perceived deformities or use of assistive devices leads to assumptions that they are less capable of attracting people or engaging in sexual activity. Wheelchair users such as Black R&B star Teddy Pendergrass and singer Connie Boswell, a white woman who survived polio, had to negotiate the disjunction between pop glamour and their supposedly unattractive or nonfunctional bodies. Their approaches were shaped by race and gender: Pendergrass's presentation as a masculine R&B lover man transitioned into his promotion as an inspirational figure of perseverance after an accident left him paralyzed, while Boswell (a member of the pioneering jazz-pop group the Boswell Sisters) variously attempted to obscure and acknowledge her wheelchair use throughout her career in an attempt to maintain an image as sexually appealing.[20] In general, musicians with noticeable physical differences either subsumed sexual desire beneath a narrative of inspiration, or obscured disability in an attempt to maintain their attractiveness with an image-focused pop marketplace. And in an ableist, racist, and sexist world, those are legitimate responses.

Ian Dury took a different approach, which renders him, despite his stylistic difference and whiteness, Bushwick Bill's clearest predecessor in the pop era. As the musicologist George McKay writes, Dury, a British artist who scored several hits during the punk and New Wave era, "produced a remarkable and sustained body of work that explored issues of disability in both personal and social contexts."[21] Dury had polio as a child, used a cane throughout his life, and had a slight build. Punk's rejection of the normal—including as it related to physical appearance—suited Dury's shorter frame, strange posture, and weakened left arm, which he proudly displayed with sleeveless shirts. And the music's spirit of outrageousness gave Dury space to record songs about sex that he delivered with a winking leer. Offering what McKay identifies as a "cluster of masculine identities," Dury's flirty filth emphasized, rather than elided, the relationship between his sexuality and his abnormal physicality.[22]

Not everybody was into it. Initially Dury faced resistance from record companies because they didn't believe that someone who looked like him could become a star. After he did, he had to deal with their anxieties about acceptable behavior.[23] "Dury's decision to appear in the video for the chart-topping single 'Hit Me With Your Rhythm Stick' in 1979 without a jacket—hence displaying his withered arm," McKay notes, "sparked a panic" at Stiff Records, despite its reputation as one of the most adventurous punk labels.[24] And his provocative "Spasticus Autisticus," released in response to the United Nations' 1981 International Year of Disabled Persons, rejected the feel-good rhetoric of the UN project in favor of an irreverent demand for recognition.[25]

Dury's defiance centered on his refusal to adhere to respectable images being promoted by advocates as a means of gaining favor from an abled public. He faced pushback from at least one advocacy organization after "Spasticus Autisticus," and his career more broadly, resisted mainstream conventions of disability in every respect. As McKay points out, "A problem with Dury as a cultural representative of disabled people may have been [that he confirmed] something distasteful, dangerous, deviant, sexually threatening within, even inherent to, people with disabilities."[26] His "dirty-old-man-in-a-mac persona" and gleefully disreputable lyrics risked reinforcing the stereotypical categories that Joseph Straus identifies as the "Demonic Cripple" motivated by malice and the "Natural Man, brutish and uncivilized."[27]

It is in this tension that Dury is closest to Bushwick Bill. By amplifying, describing, and joking about the sex that his disabled body enjoyed, Dury, like Bill, showed how the hypervisibility of the freak show could be harnessed for subversive ends while still potentially reinforcing its most problematic assumptions. Sex was a primary way, though not the only one, in which Bill embodied McKay's observation about Dury that "his body was his book," as he "wrote autobiographical and observational lyrics about disability" that he "then performed . . . on stage."[28]

Bushwick Bill's Blackness gives additional and specific resonance to the "Natural Man, brutish and uncivilized" stereotype that his licentious rhymes invoke. The linkage between race and disability placed him in a history extending from slavery's objectifications to Barnum's racist ballyhoo to the experiences of disabled musicians from Blind Tom forward. But his Blackness also placed Bill in a cultural tradition through which popular music became a central site of resistance, a strain of assertion that had been foregrounded in rap music since its beginnings, which he had witnessed firsthand. In the late 1980s, with both N.W.A. and Public Enemy as new referents, hip-hop's brash lyrics, explosive sound, and outsized performers offered Bushwick Bill fertile ground to expose and exploit ableist and racist legacies.

He brought this history with him even when he appeared as a dancer at early Geto Boys shows, but "Size Ain't Shit" was his chance to speak in provocative and profane detail. As the only short rapper in the game, there was nobody else like him, and he made his dwarfism impossible to ignore. Silent no more, Bushwick Bill would now be louder than a bomb.

"SIZE AIN'T SHIT"

"Size Ain't Shit" opens with an invitation and a challenge. DJ Ready Red asks Bushwick Bill to tell us how he responds when "motherfuckers underestimate [his] size." Over a blast of rhythm he responds, "First of all, I laugh," then details the ways that his shortness shouldn't fool any clowns into thinking that he's not sexually prolific, or capable of violence in either self-defense or aggression, or (in all respects, including some problematic ones) as much of a man as anyone else.

Bill explains his romantic exploits in detail, noting that his shortness is an asset, not a liability: "And while you're gettin' on your knees to fuck, a nigga like me is still standin' up." He also suggests that his literal and figurative manhood renders any concerns moot. "I'll show your girl how a real man feels," he promises. "Large things come in very small packages." The belt-notch braggadocio and big-dick energy then transitions into a gleeful promise of payback to anyone who disrespects him, whether those offenses come through insulting comments or manhandling. "Liftin' weights will make you bigger, but lift me, you'll be a dead-ass nigga," he spits, making a dead-serious reference to the odious practice of dwarf-tossing. Crafted by Willie D from Bill's recollections, the lyrics of "Size Ain't Shit" are outrageous, evocative, and occasionally hilarious. Over an insistent Fred Wesley sample and a splattering drum track, Bill delivers these lyrics with a blistering flow that recalls the work of both emcees from his beloved Public Enemy, mixing the poised precision of Chuck D with the reckless abandon of Flavor Flav. In every respect, it's a tour de force.

"Size Ain't Shit" is a standout track on 1989's *Grip It! On That Other Level*. It was the breakthrough album for the Ghetto Boys (who changed the spelling to "Geto" after the album's release), and it was the first with their classic lineup: Scarface, Willie D, and a fully operational Bushwick Bill joining DJ Ready Red. As Rolf Potts notes, "Size Ain't Shit" was both a "clever branding gesture" and a "hyperbolic MC mission statement that announces [Bill's] transition from being the group's smallest backup dancer to its most outsized and flamboyantly recognizable personality."[1] It established a theme, tone, and language that he used to defy ableist stereotypes, assert his masculinity, and generally hype himself. "Size Ain't Shit" announced the worldview that Bushwick Bill rapped about throughout his career.

"Size Ain't Shit" is not a traditional empowerment anthem. It makes no mention of a political program, nor does it call for greater acceptance. What makes it groundbreak-

-42-

ing, beyond its sheer existence, is its joyous and uncompromised celebration of being short in a context where it had largely been presented as a sign of deficiency. When shortness appears as subject matter in pop music, it's either comical, like the winking geniality of Little Jimmy Dickens and lazy midget jokes, or tragic. In songs across eras and genres, being physically small is a favorite metaphor for how full-sized folks (especially men, and especially in relation to love or sex) become diminished. Add in related images such as "half a man," "cut me down to size," and others, and the metaphor of shortness to signal downfall or emasculation is surprisingly ubiquitous. These tropes connect to larger cultural perceptions of short-statured people. "Even within the normal range, shortness has signaled immaturity and powerlessness," David Gerber notes. "When coupled with the bodily disproportions common to many dwarfs, furthermore, shortness has been regarded as grotesque and has been an even more likely cause for ridicule and mocking, if at times also affectionate, humor."[2] The most prominent pop precursor to "Size Ain't Shit" worked all these angles.

In 1977, Randy Newman released "Short People," which became a surprise Top 10 hit for the respected singer-songwriter. Released from his album *Little Criminals*, the jaunty earworm presents a protagonist who says that short people have "no reason to live" and "nobody to love." The verses describe a litany of reasons (from "grubby little fingers" to "dirty little minds") before declaring in a sing-along chorus, "I don't want no short people 'round here." Given its chart performance and the scarcity of competitors, "Short People" is the most successful song about shortness in pop history, a rather ironic achievement given that Newman himself is nearly six feet tall.

It was clearly meant to be a gag, an acid-tipped satire from an artist well known for unsympathetic narrators. It pokes fun not only at the bigotry of its protagonist but also at the "all men are brothers" cliché that defines so much of the era's pop-rock politics. Newman himself later said that the narrator "is not to be believed," and it's pretty clear that he felt no warmer toward him than he did for the slave trader of his song "Sail Away."[3] The song's central joke has never bothered me, and though I reflexively wince at the references to "little feet," "little voices," and the like, I don't believe that Newman intended for this to be anything other than more sweetly delivered poison from a fundamentally humane songwriter. (Although I do wish that his performance of the song on *Saturday Night Live* hadn't included the background singers kneeling down for the final chorus. Ha fuckin' ha.)

Artistic intent does not, however, equal audience reception, and the popularity of "Short People" made it controversial. It was banned from numerous radio stations, and Newman's concerts were picketed by activists.[4] Some who criticized the song didn't get it, mistaking Newman's ironic wit for sincere mockery. But even many of those who understood Newman's meaning also recognized the potential effect of a cheery denunciation of short people (even if it was ironic) in a period when those same folks were organizing to gain greater social acceptance and even political strength.

One of the key components of that response was the national organization Little People of America, which condemned "Short People" as part of a larger campaign to broaden opportunities and gain respect. "The magnitude of the historic difference that the growth of LPA made in the lives of dwarfs cannot be overstated," Betty Adelson suggests, especially because "media attention to the organization has increased public awareness and inspired social change."[5] The group began primarily as an advocacy organization for entertainers who sought to avoid demeaning roles, and it more generally promoted an image of people with dwarfism as productive and respectable members of society, a "just like you" message that they used to fight discrimination in employment, culture, and elsewhere. They encouraged what David Gerber calls "self-worth" among short-statured people, pushing back against "the psychological consequences of stigmatization" and social consequences, including the participation of dwarfs in "debasement" through demeaning activities.[6] In all respects, the LPA aimed to diminish negative representations, whether produced by outsiders or involving members of the community themselves.[7] In a sense, then, Bushwick Bill defied both "Short People" and the LPA with "Size Ain't Shit" by refusing to view shortness as a deficit and by insisting that his shortness made him *better* than you, and not just in safe or acceptable ways.

The crudeness of "Size Ain't Shit" is not unproblematic. The numerous references to penis size and the shared imagery he uses to describe sex and violence uncomfortably suggest the historical notion that Black people (particularly men) are exceptionally and violently sexual, a lie used to justify everything from segregation to slavery to lynching.[8] The song contains sexist and homophobic language, as well as a suggestion that violence, even when cartoonish, is a workable solution to most problems. And Bill's excesses risked overcorrection in his attempt to erase what Rebecca Adelman calls the image of the "bitter-emasculated-cripple" by turning himself into the "triumphant-hyper-masculine cripple" that often serves as the only alternative.[9] But in all its gross and glorious excess, "Size Ain't Shit" offers not only a uniquely detailed description of life from the perspective of a short person but also, crucially, the perspective of a short person who doesn't give a fuck what you think about it.

The unruly persona that Bill explores in "Size Ain't Shit" recurs throughout his other contributions to *Grip It!*. The album rebooted the Ghetto Boys, moving away from the derivative Run-DMC mimicry of *Making Trouble* by introducing new group members and the now-trademark mix of provocative rhymes, boisterous interplay, and sonic clatter that reflected the influence of N.W.A., Public Enemy, and others while asserting a uniquely Houston musical and lyrical approach. "The music was hard. The lyrics was dark, borderline scary," James Prince recalled. "But I knew we had something."[10] Bushwick Bill doesn't appear on every track, but he stood at the center of the storm and became the mouthpiece for many of the most incendiary lyrics.

In fact, after barely appearing on the previous album, Bill is the first rapper you hear on *Grip It!*. "I'm back like a rebel 'making trouble,' I'm an assassin, kickin' ass on the double," he declares in the opening verse of "Do It Like a G.O.," referencing the first album and its most enduring lyric: "No motherfucker alive's gonna stop me, so fuck you and your goddamn posse." Over a propulsive Curtis Mayfield sample, "Do It Like a G.O." extends its taunts beyond the assumed targets. Here, the "goddamn posse" also includes those who would shut down rap music while tolerating or promoting atrocities. Willie D noted the destructive power of the global drug trade, Scarface slammed educational racism, and both men attacked the racism of a record industry that promoted only New York rap and wouldn't play the Geto Boys on the radio.

Bushwick Bill's verse on "G.O." only glances at politics, but his is the primary voice of resistance on the album's most eloquent polemic, "Talking Loud Ain't Saying Nothin'." Remixing the James Brown track that provides the song's title, Bushwick Bill's verse aims straight at late '80s culture wars. By the end of the decade, rap artists and audiences faced increasing criticism as their records gained larger audiences (particularly among younger white people) and offered more extreme and confrontational messages. Singled out for repression, Bushwick Bill pointed out the hypocrisy of "goddamn parents" who would try to prevent kids from hearing rap and yet "take 'em to the movies to watch Schwarzenegger." Noting the "goddamn hypocrite[s]" who "curse worse than me" yet protest the group, Bill pointed out that this literal and figurative policing contrasts with the American dream of upward mobility: "Fuck that 'land of opportunity' shit."

The use of Hollywood movies to expose a moralist double standard became one of the Geto Boys' primary rhetorical weapons as they compared their fiendish fantasies to hit movies that featured graphic sex and violence. And such a defense was necessary given the contents of the album's closing tracks, "Trigga Happy Nigga" and "Mind of a Lunatic." More than any of the other tracks on *Grip It!*, these two songs embody the group's new hardcore approach, and although both Scarface and Willie D offer compelling verses, the most memorable, and problematic, parts of each song belong to Bushwick Bill. After being absent for the five songs following "Size Ain't Shit," a stretch that not coincidentally feels most like a throwback to *Making Trouble*, Bushwick Bill returns to take the Geto Boys over the edge.

"Trigga Happy Nigga" opens with a sample and invocation of King Curtis's celebratory 1960s hit "Memphis Soul Stew" but then incorporates references to the intoxicating ingredients of Houston rap. "Today's special is ghetto dope processed in Fifth Ward Texas," says group associate Lil' J, including "an ounce of Fifth Ward bass" and "a key of uncut drums" ready to be processed and sold by the Geto Boys. The joyous introduction gives way to a deranged lyric. On the first two verses, Scarface and Willie D present stories that end in bloodshed. But Bill's final verse is easily the most intense because he introduces the threat of sexual coercion. He describes robbing a liquor store, where he beats up a female employee who offers to have sex with him if he will leave her alone. Bill recognizes that she's just trying to stall for the police, who will likely kill him rather than take him to jail, so he takes the money and gets away. Intriguingly, Bill's is the only narrator who doesn't kill anyone. Beyond that, he doesn't have sex with the clerk, in part because he recognizes the looming reality of police violence. Bill presents all this as restraint, and while the verse is brutal and misogynist, it complicates the supposedly "trigga happy" recklessness that drives the song and propelled criticism of the Geto Boys and their gangsta counterparts.

All restraints are absent in the over-the-top nightmare of "Mind of a Lunatic." Over rumbling funk and a low guitar riff, sampled from a recording by James Brown's band the J.B.'s, the Geto Boys dive even deeper into their ultraviolent storytelling. Bushwick Bill again delivers the most horrific rhymes, opening the song by describing the rape and murder of a woman in her home. Even in the most generous interpretation, it's a deeply troubling lyric that was used, fairly, to condemn the group for its easy deployment of sexual violence as a scare tactic.

It was also used unfairly as a supposed demonstration of the group's depravity, despite the fact that it is framed as both nightmarish fiction and a cautionary tale. It describes vile behavior from messed-up characters that we aren't meant to identify with, and who end up dead or in jail because of their crimes. It nods toward mental illness and drug use; the song's first word is "paranoid," rapped by Bill in a near scream, and all three members address their delusional states as explanation, but not justification, for their crimes. With its references to both Jason and Freddy Krueger, the song draws a connection to horror films while implicitly suggesting its relationship to the horror shows going on outside of rap culture. After the narrator kills and rapes his victim, he notices the TV is on and calls it a "witness" to his crimes. When the police arrive, Bill asks the audience (and perhaps himself) if he should "live in reality" or "live in the television."[11] By forcing his audience to consider the blurry line between fact and fiction, and their own relationship to it as spectators, Bushwick Bill established a duality that characterized the Geto Boys' work as they grew in fame and infamy.

By introducing the "Mind of a Lunatic," Bushwick Bill and the Geto Boys also confronted discourses of insanity that had long been weaponized against Black Americans. From the phony condition of "drapetomania," which was blamed for slave escapes, to the use of diagnoses of schizo-phrenia to pathologize and imprison protestors during the civil rights movement, claims of craziness structured white dismissals of Black defiance as irrational and danger-ous.[12] Notions of lunacy informed the relationship of Afri-can Americans to the criminal justice system through both imprisonment and involuntary institutionalization.[13] And white stereotypes, including those that fueled freak shows and blackface minstrelsy, often framed Black actions as in-explicable products of uncontrollable impulses. In all its bizarre brutality, "Mind of a Lunatic" both mirrored and confounded those narratives.

The song also offered the Geto Boys' first contribution to the history of Black cultural responses to these discourses. Black artists have often used perceptions of insanity as sub-version — including the masked mischief of slavery's trick-ster tales, which feature figures whose seemingly foolish or irrational behavior conceals insight that helps them outwit those with more physical or social power — as do their de-scendants in blues, comedy, and other forms.[14] Black cre-ators have also argued that insanity is a serious, under-standable by-product of living in a cruel and racist society, even if it leads to violent crimes (like those committed by Bigger Thomas in Richard Wright's influential novel *Native Son*) or the internal turmoil documented by devil-hounded blues narrators. As hip-hop legends Grandmaster Flash and the Furious 5 reminded listeners in their founda-tional 1982 track "The Message," MC Melle Mel was "trying not to lose my head" in a crazy-making world around him.

Indeed, starting with "Mind of a Lunatic," the Geto Boys engaged these tropes in a manner that bespoke their larger saliency among hip-hop artists. The group "contributed to the commonplace rhetorical practice in rap music of claiming to be mentally ill for a two-fold meaning," argues Mikko Koivisto, "first, as a reference to one's aptness to engage in violence and crime; and second, to be able to produce excessively violent lyrical content."[15] But, thanks to Bushwick Bill, the subversive trickery existed as well. Numerous rappers adopted personas that suggested eccentricity or neurodivergence; in a group context, such as Ol' Dirty Bastard in Wu-Tang Clan or Flavor Flav in Public Enemy, the presence of such performers offers a chaotic counterpoint to headier or more straightforward lyricists, while their buggin'-out personas allow them to explore otherwise unavailable territory. If "Size Ain't Shit" was the trickster's laugh, "Mind of a Lunatic" was its horror-scream counterpart.

It's worth noting that, just as Willie D wrote the lyrics to "Size Ain't Shit," Bill's verses on "Mind of a Lunatic" and many other Geto Boys tracks were composed by others. Prominent rappers have used credited and uncredited writers over the years, and collaborative record-making has been significant throughout hip-hop history, but Bushwick Bill's reliance on other lyricists may suggest that his legacy deserves an asterisk. But there are several ways in which Bill's use of writers doesn't reduce his accomplishments. For one thing, those who wrote lyrics for and with him stylized them to his particular gifts; for example, there's no way that Willie D would have composed "Size Ain't Shit" if he hadn't been working with Bill. Additionally, even in verses that are less specific to his life, Bushwick's exceptional persona and "extraordinary body" gave the words unique meaning. This can be unsettling, especially when lyrics chosen for Bill were the vilest or most extreme, thus suggesting the grotesque side of the freak show. But no matter which (or whose) lyrics he was rhyming, Richard Shaw developed the character of Bushwick Bill across three decades of songs and albums, including an eventual solo career where he rhymed without the use of collaborators. In both sound and concept, his voice was his own.

Grip It! earned significant national attention. It got a rave review in the preeminent hip-hop magazine, *The Source*, and rose to No. 19 on the *Billboard* R&B/hip-hop chart. The album even reached the lower reaches of the main *Billboard* album chart, reaching No. 156, an impressive achievement given its independent roots and the consistent undercounting of rap albums before the introduction of SoundScan technology in 1991. The first rap album from Houston to hit nationally, *Grip It!* was a triumph for Rap-a-Lot Records and a breakthrough for the city. The Geto Boys, and Houston hip-hop, had arrived.

Among the album's fans was producer Rick Rubin,

whose booming productions and fuck-you sneer helped establish Def Jam Records as one of rap's premier labels in the 1980s. (His productions for Run-DMC were a key influence on *Making Trouble*.) After leaving Def Jam, Rubin partnered with the major label Geffen Records to distribute his new Def American imprint, which would specialize in the hardcore sounds that he loved in rap and heavy metal. The Geto Boys seemed like a perfect candidate for Def American. "Rick was anti-establishment, and he liked the fact that we didn't hold back lyrically," James Prince remembered. "He wanted to add to our movement."[16] The Geto Boys signed with Rubin in late 1989.

Rather than record an entirely new album, Rubin reconfigured and re-released *Grip It!* as their 1990 major label debut, simply titled *Geto Boys*. He remixed and re-recorded tracks from the album (along with "Assassins" from *Making Trouble*), including fuller productions, new vocal tracks, and small modifications to lyrics and arrangements. The tracks were reordered ("Size Ain't Shit" was the second, and the first to showcase a single rapper), and the group recorded new spoken intros where they talked about the importance of Black-owned record companies and the continued annoyance of protests by parents. They also recorded a couple of new tracks in response to their growing notoriety.

The most notable change was the additional appearances of Bushwick Bill, including on songs previously released without his involvement. He shows up on the playful

"Gangster of Love," affirming his reputation as an unexpectedly powerful lover, but his other new contributions were among the record's most violent lyrics. On "Assassins," Bill raps the third and most extreme verse. Originally rhymed by Johnny C, it includes descriptions of killing his father and having sex with a woman only to find out that she gave him AIDS, then shooting her in the back and dismembering the corpse. He frames it as fiction by referencing the movie *Texas Chainsaw Massacre*, but it's nasty regardless of its debatable sincerity. And on the new version of "Mind of a Lunatic," the already nightmarish third verse gets even darker. "Bushwick Bill's narrator had previously fretted about the cops after slitting his victim's throat," Rolf Potts describes, "where now we see him having sex with the corpse, smearing his name on to the wall in the victim's blood" in the style of the Manson Family, "and calling the cops on himself."[17] Coming directly after "Size Ain't Shit," the new "Mind of a Lunatic" emphasized Bill's importance to the group and Rick Rubin's vision for them.

Even as Bushwick Bill seared himself into a listener's consciousness, the use of him on this album has a troubling undertone. Rolf Potts notes that "Bushwick Bill's psycho-dwarf persona" became crucial to Rubin's plan for the Geto Boys, so he made Bill into its primary provocateur.[18] If the use of Bushwick Bill to deliver the most extreme rhymes on *Grip It!* had already invoked freak-show spectacle, now that process was being directed, Barnum-style, by a white producer interested in creating a cultural shit storm from which he could profit. Even allowing for the group's participation in creating these outrageous rhymes, and further acknowledging the scorching performances, the use of a physically different Black body (the only one pictured shirtless on the album cover) in this way recalls the freak show's particular commodification of disabled Black people.

This queasiness is one reason Bill's presence on the album's new political songs is so important. The opening and closing tracks frame the album's outrageous contents as a confrontation with injustice and hypocrisy. First comes "Fuck 'Em," an explosive takedown of the haters and imitators. Using a Jamaican patois that recalls his youth, Bill's verse notes the group's role in putting Houston on the map even as they fought with teachers who hated them and media organizations that claimed they wouldn't make it. The album's last track, "City Under Siege," returns to Houston in the age of the war on drugs. Opening with a cocaine-centric riff on the Coca-Cola jingle "I'd Like to Teach the World to Sing," it contrasts Scarface mythology (both the Pacino movie and Brad Jordan's persona) with the realities of cocaine as a global commodity and street-level mechanism for Black poverty and racist policing. In his verse, Bushwick Bill notes that "They don't care about niggas on welfare, as long as their kind ain't there" and invokes the killing of an unarmed Black woman in Houston as a word of warning to crooked cops: "You won't get a chance to slay me. I won't be an accident like Ida Delaney."[19] Defending oneself in a "city under siege" offers a different view of the criminal characters explored earlier, ending *Geto Boys* on a note of weighty anger, and Bill proves as crucial to these tracks as to their sensationalistic counterparts.

Pleased with the results, Rubin submitted the album to Geffen Records and awaited the inevitable controversy. It didn't take long to arrive. The album's contents raised concerns within the company's leadership, who worried that it would alienate customers and agitate lawmakers. But the shit really hit the fan when someone at an Indiana factory heard Bushwick Bill's verse on "Mind of a Lunatic" while they were producing copies of the CD. Horrified, they refused to print any more, and Geffen reconsidered its decision to release the album.

The Geto Boys were not the first hip-hop group to inspire such consternation, but this moment signaled their arrival as a flashpoint in larger battles over rap and its cultural consequences, a role they held throughout the 1990s. Bushwick Bill became the group's most prominent member, held up as a specific target for both pillory and praise, and called upon to defend the group's music. Little Billy may have started as a sideshow, but Bushwick Bill was about to become a spokesman.

CAN'T BE STOPPED

In September 1990, former New York mayor Ed Koch devoted his syndicated newspaper column to cultural degeneration in the United States. "It's gotten to the point," Koch claimed, "where it seems that the only art worthy of attention in the minds of some in the art community is art that goes out of its way to be sexually, racially or socially offensive." Koch cited numerous well-known firestorms from the period, including Andres Serrano's "Piss Christ" and Sinead O'Connor's refusal to sing if "The Star-Spangled Banner" was played prior to her performance. But Koch saved his greatest ire for the Geto Boys, whom he mocked as "the latest standard bearers of the Constitution and heroes of the art world." Noting that their current album was being held back by Geffen Records, Koch quoted "sickening lyrics" from two songs as reasons why it deserved to be kept from listeners. One of them was Bushwick Bill's verse on "Mind of a Lunatic."[1]

Koch was also angered by Bushwick Bill's public statements. Quoting a *New York Times* interview with Jon Pareles, Koch repeated Bill's claims that the group's rhymes reflected a reality that America was choosing to ignore. "We were just expressing stuff that happens in the ghetto, just like being reporters," Bill told Pareles. "We want to make everybody mad enough to look at the ghetto right in their own state, not just to look at the middle-class and the rich areas."[2] Koch was unconvinced: "Is Geffen Records required to distribute this 'reportage' which surely at best is misogynist and at worst a call for rape and mayhem? No." Applauding Geffen for exercising "private censorship," Koch asked his fellow anxious Americans, "Is there any wonder that there is so much violence in the streets of our cities?"[3]

Koch's column was an early illustration of the trend that placed the Geto Boys at the center of controversies over rap music and the cultural decline it supposedly represented. The group joined counterparts like 2 Live Crew, Ice-T, and Tupac Shakur in earning condemnation from a unique coalition of conservative politicians, so-called moral authorities, and former civil rights activists who viewed these groups' music as promoting violence, misogyny, and dangerous behavior. This coalition—which bridged partisan, racial, and generational lines—urged parents, concerned citizens, the recording industry, and even Congress to keep the music away from impressionable young people and instead promote more positive messages. As Koch's comments demonstrated, Bushwick Bill's contributions to "Mind of a Lunatic" became one of the most oft-cited texts used by this coalition to demonstrate their case. The song's supposedly unspeakable lyrics were recited and reprinted for shocked audiences throughout the 1990s.

Bushwick Bill became the group's primary representative in those years. "He was the voice for the Geto Boys," James Prince recalled. "I had him speak to the press the way I'm doing right now. I can send a message through him, and it wouldn't get messed up too bad. He knew how to deliver."[4] Bill spoke out in defense of the group and its fans, condemning the hypocrisy of self-appointed culture warriors and calling out the deeper problems more deserving of their attention. This did not always go well, particularly when Bill's sexist comments confirmed critiques of Black women who pushed back against rap's misogyny. But Bushwick Bill symbolized the pushback that earned the group (sometimes grudging) support from free speech advocates and others who viewed the group as necessary voices in the conversation. "They can't hold us back," Bushwick Bill assured Jon Pareles. "The truth can't be stopped."[5]

Bill articulated the Geto Boys' position on several battlefields in what Tricia Rose calls "the hip-hop wars."[6] The group recognized that many attacks on their recordings were motivated by larger anxieties over the state of young Black America in the post–civil rights backlash of the Reagan era. And they played a complex role in debates over the treatment of women in rap and the broader demonization of Black women in an era stretching from Reagan's "welfare queens" to Clinton's welfare reform. Whether eloquently laying out the facts of US politics or using sexist language in response to legitimate questions from Black women, Bushwick Bill—once a freaky novelty—became a key figure in American cultural politics.

He did this both despite and because of his unique physicality. His stature was routinely mentioned, often without context, by writers trying to describe the Geto Boys for their readers. Sometimes his size was used to explain his outrageous behavior by both his fans and detractors, demonstrating Rosemarie Garland-Thomson's insight that "the physically disabled body becomes a repository for social anxieties about such troubling concerns as vulnerability, control, and identity."[7] Just as freak shows had crystallized societal fears a century earlier, Bushwick Bill's disruptive appearance crystallized the supposedly degenerative (or was it disabling?) effect of hardcore rap. As one writer put it in 1990, "Next time Tipper Gore or any of the other anti-rock Blue Meanies need a good example of a bad example, they need look no further than the Geto Boys. On its self-titled major-label debut, this Houston rap group—led by a sinister dwarf—makes 2 Live Crew look like The Brady Bunch."[8]

The work of the "sinister dwarf" bespoke a parallel connection. The Geto Boys also emerged alongside the passage of the Americans with Disabilities Act, signed by President George H. W. Bush in 1990. The ADA symbolized a victory for the disability rights movement, which emerged in the 1970s and forced legislation like the ADA through direct action and political pressure. Building on the earlier Rehabilitation Act, the ADA expanded protections against discrimination in employment, housing, and education and required a wide-ranging set of accommodations ranging from building codes to public transportation.

The passage of the ADA also seemed to symbolize the cultural acceptance of disabled people, even if that acceptance was mostly framed through the same lens of "just like you" respectability or "overcomer" sentimentality. But even that victory was often represented only through images of white people, despite the key roles of Black activists in forcing the passage of legislation, part of a larger erasure of the Black contribution to disability activism.[9] Although limited in its scope, hard to enforce, and under constant challenge from the right wing, the ADA was a crucial breakthrough. I'm only one of the many whose lives were transformed, and made possible, because of it. Bushwick Bill never publicly commented on the ADA, but his concurrent role as an outspoken, unruly, and disabled Black person in the public eye offered loud confirmation of disabled assertion and a disruptive counterpoint to the mythical acceptance meant to follow in the ADA's wake.

Geffen Records tried to preempt controversy over *Geto Boys* by embracing the primary weapon deployed by censors in the late 1980s. They would include not only the Parental Advisory sticker that the record industry had adopted in response to the demands of the Parents Music Resource Center (PMRC), but also a Geffen-specific version that declaimed any official condoning of the album's content.[10] The disclaimers didn't prevent outrage from some of the album's first and most influential listeners: the staff of the Indiana-based factory contracted by Geffen to manufacture *Geto Boys* discs. The company refused to press the CDs, forcing Geffen to scramble to find a new distributor as early copies were sent to critics and the lead single, "Do It Like a G.O.," was released as both a recording and a video.

As Jon Pareles notes, "Do It Like a G.O." is "about fighting racism" rather than the lurid gore that had supposedly caused offense.[11] But the political critiques did not stanch concern over the violent and sexual content of the album; in fact, it's likely that the group's assertive Blackness further angered many of its detractors, so the label pulled the album at the last minute. "I've never been frightened by a record before in my life," Geffen executive Bryn Birdenthal claimed at the time, "but for me the graphic details of the violence were really frightening."[12] As Bill later noted, the Geto Boys became "the first group in the history of music to ever be banned from manufacturing. 2 Live Crew was manufactured and was banned for being stocked in the stores."[13]

Bill's reference to the Miami group was poignant and appropriate. The previous year, the release of 2 Live Crew's album *As Nasty As They Wanna Be* led to the arrest of group members and record store owners in Orlando, Florida, by prosecutor Jack Thompson. The group's breakthrough paralleled and intersected with that of the Geto Boys. Each established their cities as rap hot spots, with distinctive sounds and independent labels that put Houston and Miami on the map. Both groups are considered key architects of Dirty South hip-hop as a musical and commercial force. And when each broke nationally, they were celebrated and censored for their provocative content.

Geffen's response to the Geto Boys was likely motivated by what happened with 2 Live Crew, but one executive, Bryn Birdenthal, suggested that the two were not comparable. "I was flabbergasted that people would describe violence that graphically in music," she told the Associated Press. "People will think this is like 2 Live Crew, which is just kind of silly, pure sex."[14] Jack Thompson took up the cause as well, including the Geto Boys' songs in his larger campaign against rap. "With the help of a compact disc player," noted Sara Rimer in a profile of the attorney, "he transcribes song lyrics he finds obscene. He then sends them by facsimile machine to record companies, reporters, law-enforcement officials and politicians."[15]

The Geto Boys also came into the crosshairs of the PMRC, the Tipper Gore–led organization whose campaign against "filthy" content in pop had produced the Parental Advisory stickers that would be placed on every album in the Geto Boys discography. According to Willie D, the group took particular umbrage at "Mind of a Lunatic": "We were doing 'Mind of a Lunatic' at the Palladium in New York in 1990. . . . At the time, that was a very controversial song with the PMRC and had Tipper Gore coming after us. They didn't like the song, so we got a lot of press about that and as soon as they said 'From Houston, Texas, The Geto Boys,' 'BOOOOOOOOO, Get the fuck off the stage!' They were booing us so long that they were booing us in shifts."[16]

Facing external and internal resistance, Geffen Records halted the album's release. Their decision earned cheers from Ed Koch, but also from Francoise Jacobsohn, president of the New York chapter of the National Organization for Women, who echoed the belief that the album "perpetuates and makes acceptable certain violence against women. We think that is abhorrent."[17] To her credit, Jacobsohn widened her target beyond the Geto Boys, noting that Geffen continued to promote white comedian Andrew "Dice" Clay, whose sexist and X-rated albums were a major seller released by Rubin's Def American subsidiary.

Clay's recordings became a key point in the criticism of Geffen's decision. "There are people who curse worse than me and hide it all," Bushwick Bill said after Geffen shelved the album, "but I ain't no hypocrite."[18] Def Jam's publicist Bill Adler (who had denounced the Geto Boys' lyrics) and 2 Live Crew's publicist Debbie Bennett both noted this hypocrisy, as did the group themselves, who pointed out that Def American also released hardcore heavy metal.[19] "They were fine with distributing satanic metal bands like Slayer," James Prince recalled, "but considered us too offensive."[20] Geffen's biggest act, Guns N' Roses, was mentioned as another sign of the label's hypocrisy since their offensive lyrics, including racist and homophobic slurs in "One in a Million," had not earned a similar rebuke.

The censorship of the Geto Boys brought them into alliance with the era's political rap even as some within that scene criticized the group for their lyrics.[21] Their silencing earned them the public support of not only Bill Adler but also Public Enemy's spokesman, Harry Allen, who addressed the controversy in *Spin*: "There's no way to exaggerate the present level of attack against African men, i.e. all hip hop music," he noted. Referencing Guns N' Roses, he pointed out that "the fact that the Geto Boys would be Geffen's pride and joy right now had they been white . . . is the least remarkable fact of this attack."[22]

The Geto Boys appreciated but did not require the assistance. They had pointed out the double standard throughout their records, noting violent Hollywood icons such as Freddy Krueger and Arnold Schwarzenegger, as well as the brutality of US policy both at home and abroad. When Geffen's decision hit the press, Bushwick Bill made this duplicity a consistent talking point. "To some reporters," Rolf Potts explained, "Bushwick would suggest that the violence on *The Geto Boys* was a sober documentary depiction of life in Houston's Fifth Ward," while elsewhere "Bushwick would cite President Bush's plans to send thousands of young Americans to war in Iraq" and the "three-fifths" clause of the US Constitution.[23]

Bill invoked both realism and fiction in defense of the

group's recordings. "I'm not any more sexist, racist or violent than the world around me," he told Greg Kot of the *Chicago Tribune*. "I just look out the window and it's the 11 o'clock news."[24] He criticized Black and white political establishments, telling Jimmy Magahern of the *San Francisco Examiner* that the Geto Boys "were speaking for the people in the ghetto who don't know what the NAACP is" and noting that both Reagan and Bush built their political careers out of the nefarious activities of the FBI and CIA.[25] Connecting international, national, local, and personal, Bill suggested that the Geto Boys used an exaggerated form to tell authentic truths about an unjust society. "We're holding a mirror up to America, and letting them see their naked selves," he told Kot. "Who knows what evil lurks in the hearts of men? That's the mirror we're holding up."[26]

This combination of rhetorical tactics defined the larger rap response to the crackdowns. As the Geto Boys were being targeted by politicians and parent groups, artists such as the LA gangsta godfather Ice-T and Luther Campbell of 2 Live Crew were arguing that rappers deserved the same consideration as any other artists creating outrageous fictions, while also claiming that their rhymes represented real-life experiences that were otherwise ignored. In addition, the key artists of the era's politicized hip-hop, including Public Enemy and former NWA member Ice Cube, argued that attacks on the music were themselves manifestations of historical racism, and rappers were becoming another example of white America's attempts to re-press Black people. While not often considered a political group, the Geto Boys made this argument central to their music from the beginning, and Bushwick Bill articulated it for those who didn't (or couldn't) hear the records.

Angered by Geffen's decision to pull the album, Rick Rubin began looking for a new home not only for the Geto Boys but also for Def American. Eventually he landed with the Warner Music Group, and *The Geto Boys*, released in late 1990, became the inaugural Def American release as a Warner imprint.[27] Warner's decision to release the album was one of several that placed them in the crosshairs of the anti-rap backlash. A year later the label was pilloried by law enforcement and conservative legislators (includ-ing President George H. W. Bush) for marketing an album by Ice-T's heavy metal side project *Body Count*, which fea-tures the song "Cop Killer." The release of *The Geto Boys* previewed this maelstrom and provided evidence for those who pressured the company into turning away from gang-sta rap.

Upon the album's Warner release, Rubin courted even more controversy. He purchased an ad in *The Source* that used a lyric from "Size Ain't Shit" — "Play pussy, get fucked" — to swipe at Geffen's cowardice. The magazine had praised both *Grip It!* and the new release; *Geto Boys* got a 3.5 mic review that noted how "Rubin seems to really like Bushwick's voice" since Bill — referred to by the re-viewer as "the midget" — dominates "Gangster of Love" and appears on other tracks where he hadn't appeared before.[28] But the ad's foul language led the magazine's Virginia printer to refuse to manufacture the issue. Bushwick Bill had halted production once again, but this time there would be a compromise. "[*The Source*] would drop the headline from the advertisement," Dan Charnas explains, "and, in the next issue, run a feature on the phenomenon of 'gangster' rap to probe some of the questions provoked by the emerging subgenre."[29] That issue included a specific discussion of the Geto Boys, and Bushwick Bill again offered an uncompromising defense: "Whenever a person decides to kill somebody, and uses my album as an excuse, they're full of shit."[30]

Ironically, *Geto Boys* did not sell as well as *Grip It!*, perhaps because the backlash scared off new listeners and retailers, and perhaps because fans saw it as a retread. But the album established the group as a national force whose supporters and detractors did not fall into expected camps. As *The Source* controversy symbolized, they provoked internal debates about how they represented the rap community and Black America. They illustrated the politics of music censorship sparked by the PMRC hearings and made vivid by the 2 Live Crew arrests. And they played a subtle but important role in the cultural landscape of late 1980s racial politics. As Greil Marcus observed, referencing an infamous ad from the 1988 presidential race, the Geffen outcry "fixed [the Geto Boys], in that segment of the public imagination that was aware of their existence, as a

Willie Horton-ism, as vandals occupying the furthest extremes of capitalism and the First Amendment, as the scum of the earth."[31] The Horton ad had supported the candidacy of George Bush, who won the presidency in part thanks to its barely coded racism. As president, Bush would be a primary lyrical subject for the Geto Boys as they prepared their next album.

Right before that album came out, "Mind of a Lunatic" was blamed for a real-life killing after two teenagers were arrested for murder in Dodge City, Kansas, in July 1991. Their lawyer claimed that they had been "hypnotized" by the Geto Boys' violent lyrics, which caused them to shoot a stranger out the window of their car. "There is an imminent danger to young people getting hold of this thing," lawyer Linda Eckleman told UPI. "It can literally mesmerize you from the repeated bass sounds that come from it. The words are horrible — it's about raping and killing." The defense didn't work, just as it had failed in a similar case when metal band Judas Priest was blamed for inciting a murder in Florida, but it contributed to the Geto Boys' controversial reputation. James Prince was steadfast. "Racism is always involved when it comes to the Geto Boys," he told the UPI. "We say a lot of things that people in high places don't like and we become a target."[32]

The album *We Can't Be Stopped* (1991) turned that target around, offering what Prince called "our raw and unapologetic response to the political backlash against us."[33] Opening with the boisterous "Rebel Rap Family," *We Can't*

Be Stopped was the Geto Boys' biggest seller and most celebrated album, and it was as political and confrontational as two other albums released the same year, Public Enemy's *Apocalypse '91* and Ice Cube's *Death Certificate*. Raging at enemies from Geffen Records to Washington, DC, *We Can't Be Stopped* placed the Geto Boys' lyrical condemnations of hypocrisy and injustice against a sound that maintained the layered clatter of previous albums while reflecting the ascendance of the thick G-Funk style pioneered by Dr. Dre, a member of N.W.A. and eventually a solo artist. In *We Can't Be Stopped* the sample-heavy clatter of *Grip It!* and *Geto Boys* gives way to more streamlined arrangements built around DJ Ready Red's bouncing funk samples (including ones from gangsta touchstones Isaac Hayes and Funkadelic) and spare, bass-heavy tracks. But the group still went after its enemies without compromise. Crooked cops, racist authorities, and, problematically, trifling women all came in for condemnation, but the Geto Boys directed particular hostility toward the record industry and the Bush administration for demonizing the group. As before, and perhaps understandably given his new notoriety, Bushwick Bill voiced many of the most pointed critiques.

Just as *Geto Boys* is bookended by protest, *We Can't Be Stopped* opens and closes with direct attacks on the music business. The title track chronicles the repression of the Geto Boys through a combination of lack of radio airplay, refusals to book live shows, and threats of arrest. In his verse, Bushwick specifically references Geffen ("Can you believe those hypocrites who distribute Guns N' Roses but not our shit?") and Jack Thompson (by referencing an unnamed racist district attorney in Florida putting rappers on trial for obscenity). The album closes with "Trophy," an attack on the Grammys and other award shows for ignoring Black artists in favor of rewarding the same white favorites. This erasure gained new life in the hip-hop era. In 1989, when it was revealed that a long-awaited Grammy rap category would not be televised, the nominated groups, even comparatively milquetoast eventual winner DJ Jazzy Jeff and the Fresh Prince, boycotted the ceremony. That incident, and the award show's larger hostility to the culture, animates a track that ends with Willie D storming the Grammy stage and giving out alternative awards to the Geto Boys (who win for "Most Fuck Words in a Song") and contemporaries 2 Live Crew, Ice Cube, and Public Enemy.

Bushwick Bill doesn't appear on "Trophy," but he is the sole rapper on the album's most potent political track, "Fuck a War." Underappreciated in discussions of antiwar music, the song offers a blistering condemnation of the Persian Gulf conflict and the broader mobilization that accompanied it. The track opens with Bill finding out that he's been drafted; he literally laughs the recruiter off the phone before explaining the various reasons why he has no interest.[34] Over a mournful saxophone and drum track that subtly interpolates military cadences, Bill criticizes the racial politics of the Gulf War, where "niggas [are] on the front line" but left "way behind" when it comes to equal opportunities at home. Echoing Muhammad Ali's famous line about the Vietnam conflict, Bill notes that "the enemy is right here, G, [and] them foreigners never did shit to me." He connects it to the exploitation of the poor through military service: frontline troops often come from lower economic status and serving is connected to economic benefits, whereas privileged people can avoid service, and politicians who declare war are often wealthy and disconnected. ("I ain't gettin' my leg shot off while Bush old ass on TV playin' golf.") Bill never mentions his shortness here, even though it would likely disqualify him from combat service, but the line about losing his leg recalls how crucial disabled veterans have been to shaping the politics and perceptions of disability.[35] And he notes that the fight for "goddamn oil" will lead only to physical and psychological damage for the soldiers who were fighting while Bush and his cronies were getting rich.[36] As Willie D declares in the chorus, all of these are reasons why they "ain't going to war for a shit-talkin' president."

I don't know whether George Bush heard "Fuck a War," although, given the FBI's larger interest in hip-hop and history of surveilling dissidents, it's likely that the lyrics went into a file somewhere. But the Geto Boys kept up their condemnations of the "shit-talkin' president" on two of the new tracks attached to their 1992 compilation, *Uncut Dope*. "Damn, It Feels Good to Be a Gangsta" traces the meanings of the term *gangsta* through personal experience, community context, and systemic implication. Bushwick Bill's verse offers a Robin Hood fantasy of wealth redistribution, with him "feeding the poor and helping out with their bills." These lyrics exhibit characteristics of what Tricia Rose refers to as the "ghetto badman," which rappers deploy as "a protective shell against real unyielding and harsh social policies and physical environments," as well as what historian William Van Deburg calls the "social bandits" of Black cultural tradition.[37]

Another feature of social bandits (usually men) is that they expose the more powerful people who are the real threat. The final verse of "Damn, It Feels Good to Be a Gangsta," rapped by James Prince, the head of Rap-a-Lot, is delivered in character as President Bush. Echoing the belief that the government planted drugs in Black neighborhoods, Prince-as-Bush says that "the Mafia family is [his] real boss" and he repays them by "letting a big drug shipment through and [sending it] to the poor community, so we can bust you know who." If anyone gets wise to his racist corruption, Bush will threaten to start another war and send "a million troops to die." He's "got the world swinging from my nuts and damn it feels good to be a gangsta."

The song's video amplifies this theme and begins with Bushwick Bill in the center of the frame. It opens with a waving American flag before transitioning to a courtroom scene where the Geto Boys appear as witnesses. Although there are shots of guns and drugs, the video makes clear that what's really on trial, or should be, is police misconduct and political duplicity. In his verse, Bill leaves the witness chair and dances atop the stand as he relates his mission to help the poor, including dropping money in a Help the Homeless can as he cruises through town in his Mercedes. While these shots are fetishistic, using his shortness to emphasize the visual, they also flip the power dynamic; when Bill walks along the platform to talk to the judge, he's the one who looks down, not the judge. The video contains other such inversions; for example, Bill's line that "gangsta-ass niggas come in all shapes and colors" is paired with shots of Reagan, Richard Nixon, Oliver North, and Clarence Thomas, and when Prince-as-Bush rhymes about allowing drugs to enter the Black community, there's a shot of Bill walking by a wall where someone has spray-painted a message about where to buy drugs. These striking juxtapositions make the true villains unmistakable.

The other new song on *Uncut Dope*, "The Unseen," stands out for a different reason. On this track the group offers an angry denunciation of abortion and features some of the group's most graphic and offensive lyrics, including misogynist and homophobic slurs. Bill's verse also attacks pro-choice protestors and President Bush, who comes under fire for defending those protestors' First Amendment rights. It's an odd turn given the Geto Boys' justified attacks on Republicans for trying to shut down the speech of rappers and their audiences. But their criticism of President Bush from the right is the least noteworthy element of a song that features the Geto Boys at their most hateful.

It's unfair to assume that the group would be pro-choice due to their other seemingly left-wing politics; in fact, in the way they discuss things like capitalism and gun rights, their songs often trend toward conservatism. Also, as Tricia Rose notes, hip-hop, even so-called conscious rap, sometimes offers "the embrace of 'strict-father' brands of patriarchal masculinity" as a defense against racist attacks and a reflection of retrograde gender politics.[38] Even though a majority of disabled people support reproductive choice, the question of reproductive rights has always been fraught for them given the way that potential disabilities identified in a fetus have been cited as a justification for abortion and eugenics. But Bill makes no such connections here. As much as he elsewhere references his size, this song contains nothing that would have provided even a modicum of nuance.

The brutal language of "The Unseen" reminds us that as subversive as Bushwick Bill could be, his rhetoric could also be offensive. This song is not the only time Bill made odious remarks about women and queer people; even if one accepts (which many will not) that the lyrics of "Mind of a Lunatic" and other songs are entirely from a character's perspective, he has presented sexist and homophobic words and ideas both on the record and in interviews.[39] Bill correctly noted that people used ableist slurs against him while condemning him for sexist language, but neither his disability nor others' ableism justifies misogyny or queer-bashing. Condemnations of the Geto Boys and other artists weren't always based in racism or puritanism, an ambivalence that structured what Tricia Rose called "the hip-hop wars" in general and provoked Bushwick Bill's most significant controversy.

At the 1993 meeting of the National Association of Black Journalists (NABJ), Bill appeared on a panel discussing the politics of rap music. At one point, journalist Karyn Collins asked Bill to defend his widespread use of *bitch* and *ho* on his recordings. He responded by saying that those terms described the only kinds of women he knew growing up: a response that failed to placate Collins or the large number of attendees who agreed with her questioning. This trope was common. Tricia Rose wrote in 1994 that she had already "grown weary of defenses" in which male rappers claimed that derogatory imagery was only about the women they knew. (She doesn't mention NABJ, but it's possible that it was one of the instances she had in mind given that elsewhere she notes the Geto Boys as an example of rap's sexism.)[40] When pushed further, asked by Collins if he would describe his mother that way, Bill turned from autobiography to insult, mocking Collins's appearance and causing two hundred members of the organization to leave the hall in protest. After being confronted by NABJ president Simmel Estes-Sumpter, who called Bill "my brother" and said that she was "nobody's bitch and nobody's ho," Bill offered a non-apology. "I apologize for speaking my mind and being myself," he said. "I hope you'll find it big enough in your heart to forgive me."[41]

Bill's appearance at the NABJ meeting made national news, with journalists using the incident to illustrate the growing backlash to sexism in rap. In one striking example, white liberal columnist Ellen Goodman gave Bill the "Misogyny in Music Prize," and said, "We would send Shaw a gag but lordy, we wouldn't want to infringe on his free speech."[42] Some of the responses suggested that his size, as well as the loss of his eye in 1991, explained his comments. Beyond the dismissive descriptions of Bill as "pint-sized" and "a one-eyed midget rapper" in recaps of the event, two Black women who witnessed the incident drew a deeper comparison.[43] Rosalind Bentley noted that several NABJ members credited Bill's outburst to a "Napoleon complex," while Donna Britt suggested that it made sense that "a less-than-handsome young man who lost half his sight tussling with a woman . . . would be contemptuous of all women."[44] Bentley and Britt thus reiterated ableist conceptions by falsely suggesting that his words were justified by his appearance.

At least they tried to analyze Bill's shortness, whereas most coverage of Bushwick Bill mentioned his size only in superficial or problematic ways. There is the aforementioned invocation of Bill as a "sinister dwarf," which was echoed by others who thought of Bill's height as a vague symbol of his authenticity and implicit explanation for his hardness. In a piece decrying the Geto Boys' hate-filled music, for example, Greg Kot described Bill as "a 4-foot midget who grew up in Houston's notorious Fifth Ward, a perpetual underdog in a world ruled by pimps and drug dealers."[45] John Leland tried something similar, noting the difficulty of growing up "undersized" in Fifth Ward and describing Bill's "short arms and legs whipping frantically around his big head and truncated torso" when he dances onstage.[46]

There is a lot of this freak-show garbage, even beyond the ubiquity of the "midget" and "pint-sized" descriptors. His height was mentioned consistently, although the numbers ranged from three feet to almost five. Journalist Bill Wyman referred to Bill's "stumpy arms dangling," and famed rock critic Robert Christgau began his review of Bill's 1992 solo debut album, *Little Big Man*, by crudely signifying on racist and ableist stereotypes while ultimately reinforcing both. "Of course you have a big one, Bill," Christgau smirked. "It goes with your minority-group status—dwarves are famous for their big ones."[47] To be fair, Bushwick Bill made his shortness central to his records, including jokes about how his stature juxtaposed with the size of his dick, but the ease with which (white male) writers deployed this language suggests that they were not listening to Bill so much as staring at him. Even though they reiterated problematic ideas, Bentley and Britt at least took Bill's appearance seriously within a legitimate line of criticism about his remarks at NABJ.

The NABJ controversy inspired more than bad press. Kevin Carter described Bill's comments as "the last straw for a group of entertainment-industry women" who decided to take action. "At a recent meeting of the National Political Congress of Black Women," Carter noted, "they established an entertainment commission" that planned to "organize boycotts and lobby for legislation to combat negative images of black women in all popular culture."[48]

The National Political Congress of Black Women was led by C. Delores Tucker, who in the 1990s became the most prominent Black critic of gangsta rap. After a career of civil rights activism, Tucker led the campaign alongside prominent allies including the Reverend Calvin Butts, minister at Harlem's Abyssinian Baptist Church, and William J. Bennett, who was secretary of education under Ronald Reagan and launched a post-cabinet career as an author and moral crusader. This unlikely cohort forced a round of congressional hearings, a fresh wave of protests, and renewed pressure on record companies to stop releasing graphic and objectionable rap records. Some of their targets were new, such as second-generation gangstas Tupac Shakur and Snoop Dogg, but others were familiar. Dan Charnas notes that at a late 1993 press conference announcing her anti-rap campaign, "Tucker unearthed the lyrics for the then-three-year-old horror song by the Geto Boys, 'Mind of a Lunatic.' 'If that isn't pornography,' Tucker said, 'I don't know what is.'"[49]

In 1994, Tucker brought her cause to Congress, and both the House and Senate launched hearings on what the Senate called "violent and demeaning imagery in popular music." Convened by Illinois senator Carol Moseley-

Braun and congresswoman Cardiss Collins, both Demo-
crats and among the few Black women in the legislature,
the hearings brought together a variety of opponents (and
some defenders) of gangsta rap and other hardcore genres.
Although he did not appear at the hearings—which, given
what happened at the NABJ meeting, may have been for
the best—Bushwick Bill was invoked in both chambers
of Congress. In the House of Representatives, talk-show
host Joseph Madison cited Bill's NABJ comments as evidence of a broader decline within the Black community.
"It is just sad to think that this is how the children of the
civil rights movement end up," he lamented, given that
"their children are subjected to the glorification of violence, sexual abuse, denigrating messages about women,
and disrespect for their community in general, all in the
name of commerce."[50]

Bushwick Bill earned even more substantive mention in
the Senate. In his statement, Dr. Robert T. M. Phillips, the
deputy medical director of the American Psychiatric Association, read several examples of lyrics that the APA felt
had contributed to the "glorification" of the "violence pan-
demic" in the United States. Among the lyrics he entered
into the official record was the rape couplet from "Mind
of a Lunatic."[51] Keith Ridley, a funeral director, implored
Bushwick Bill and a list of other rappers to "stop the mad-
ness of self-hatred" and rethink their objectionable lyrics.
Later in the hearing, Nicholas Butterworth, speaking for
the nonprofit organization Rock the Vote (which had part-

nered with MTV), defended the song as "a character being portrayed" and encouraged the Senate to recognize the "nuance," "subtlety," and "irony" that younger audiences recognize and appreciate in rap's lyrics.

A year later "Mind of a Lunatic" returned as part of Tucker and Bennett's campaign against the Time Warner conglomerate. At a June 1995 press conference, Bennett rapped Bushwick's "Lunatic" verse as part of his demonstration of the degraded content peddled by the corporation, and he demanded that Warner stop distributing Interscope Records, the home of Tupac, Snoop Dogg, and others. Afterward, as *Los Angeles Times* journalist Chuck Phillips reported, "conservatives and liberals lined up to support Bennett's contention that the lyrics to the Geto Boys' rap slasher psycho-drama were disgusting and unsuitable for distribution by a major media company of Time Warner's stature." Delores Tucker also pulled out "Mind of a Lunatic" in a meeting with Time Warner executives. "Tucker not only reiterated her demand that Time Warner divest itself of Interscope," Dan Charnas described, but "she also insisted that [executives Michael] Fuchs and [Doug] Morris read the lyrics to the now five-year-old Geto Boys song, 'Mind of a Lunatic.' 'I'll give you a hundred dollars to read it!' she told Fuchs. When he refused, she stormed out of the meeting."[52]

Despite the use of "Mind of a Lunatic" to shame Warner executives, the Geto Boys hadn't been on the label for several years.[53] Phillips described the group as part of a larger cohort of rappers—including Ice-T, Paris, and Da Lench Mob—who have been "driven from Time Warner . . . following disputes over violent and sexually explicit lyrics."[54] Sensing that political convenience was behind the resurgence in criticism, Bushwick Bill wasn't having it. "My music is being condemned strictly for publicity and votes," he told Phillips in 1995. "I guess it's easier to bash rap artists than to talk about the country's real problems, such as the AIDS crisis, poverty, the cost of education, crime or the gun-toting white supremacist militias."[55]

Bill's comments were directed specifically at one of Bennett and Tucker's most ardent political admirers. Senator Bob Dole, then launching a Republican presidential campaign against Democratic incumbent Bill Clinton, took up the culture war as a key plank of his effort. Clinton had his own history of criticizing hip-hop; his public denunciation of provocative comments by Public Enemy associate Sister Souljah helped win over white moderates in the 1992 campaign against Bushwick Bill's nemesis George H. W. Bush.[56] Hoping to gain purchase with voters, in his broadsides Dole attacked everything from violent video games to explicit movies, but rap was a favorite target.

In a May 1995 speech to GOP donors, Dole mentioned the Geto Boys as purveyors of what he called the "mindless violence and loveless sex" that characterized too much of the day's pop culture.[57] He said the entertainment industry "crossed [a line] every time sexual violence is given a catchy tune," and he condemned "music which extols the pleasure of raping, torturing and mutilating women" along-side other "nightmares of depravity" from Hollywood and elsewhere. Just like Ed Koch, Bill Bennett, Delores Tucker, and others before him, Dole called on the entertainment industry to police itself and end "the mainstreaming of de-viancy" that contributed to growing social problems. As with his predecessors, Bushwick Bill's group was one of Dole's specific targets.[58]

The senator may have had personal reasons as well. In the video for Bill's July 1995 solo single, "Who's The Big-gest?," he included a shot of him burning a "Dole For Presi-dent" poster. Asked for comment, Bill's spokeswoman said that the "hip-hop community is tired of being exploited. This sends a strong message that they aren't going to be silent."[59] The Dole campaign condemned the video, saying that Bill had "reacted out of hatred." But Bill suggested that Dole had done him an unexpected favor. "I want to thank Bob Dole and all his lily-livered . . . politician homies for giving me more than $300,000 of free press" for his album. "I want to thank him for opening his mouth and sticking his foot in it so I could be heard."[60]

Just as he had unpacked the subtext beneath early 1990s conservative attacks on his music, Bill examined the cyni-cism and hypocrisy of Dole's comments. "So, this is the same man who has Senator Packwood as one of the chief executives of his campaign: who was filed [*sic*] for sexual harassment and molestation," Bill noted, and he reminded readers that Dole had voted against the restriction of semi-automatic weapons. "Now, I give one of you a Bushwick Bill tape and give the other a semi-automatic weapon, which one do you think kills? . . . So him making semi-automatic weapons available to teenagers and saying music shouldn't be heard is not only immoral, but unconstitutional." But even as he proclaimed his First Amendment rights, Bill noted that the Constitution had housed the "three-fifths" clause, which classified Black people as less than human in the eyes of the United States. "So, basically we were exempt from the Bill of Rights so F—— the government and F—— anybody that thinks I can't say what I want to say 'cause I don't give a F—— about how they feel, 'cause I'd rather be hated for who I am than loved for what I'm not."[61]

Dole's criticism invigorated Bushwick Bill's solo career. "Who's the Biggest?" appeared on 1995's *Phantom of the Rapra*, which became Bill's highest-charting solo album. In his review, Anthony De Curtis noted that Bill, "a First Amendment poster boy . . . coined the term rapra to indict the hypocrisy of people who would censor rap, even though opera deals with many of the same taboo subjects and 'rap is opera to people in the ghetto.'"[62] *The Phantom of the Rapra* not only included "Who's the Biggest?" but also "Mr. President," a timely election message that mapped the historical marginalization of Black men, from the three-fifths clause to the contemporary challenges of unfair housing and unjust policing. At the end of the song, Bill offered a gangsta remix of Malcolm X as a threat addressed to the unnamed president: If you don't pay attention to the needs of people in the ghetto, "you've offered me the right to elect you to a bullet."[63]

Dole's criticism also helped reunite the Geto Boys, who had been on hiatus following the release of *'Til Death Do Us Part* in 1993. That album, which continued the commercial success of *We Can't Be Stopped*, had been distinguished by "Crooked Officer," a hit single that re-upped the rage that drove Ice-T's "Cop Killer" and, before that, N.W.A.'s "Fuck the Police." The singsong chorus finds new member Big Mike (who temporarily replaced Willie D, who was then pursuing a solo career) threatening to put every "crooked officer . . . in a coffin, sir," and the verses ground the revenge fantasy in an assessment of conditions. On Bill's verse, he notes that "the brutality in my neighborhood is gettin' persistent," and that unlike Rodney King, Bill will react to a beating by turning the "blue shirts . . . red." While Dole and other critics would likely condemn "Crooked Officer" as "mindless violence," a closer listen reveals a more complicated picture.

The Dole attacks convinced the group to reunite and respond. Scarface remembered feeling like this "Dole muthafucka, is telling his side, so let me tell mine," so the group — with a returning Willie D, but without DJ Ready Red, who left for good over a financial dispute — returned in 1996 with *The Resurrection*. "This focus resulted in an album full of not merely scare tactics," Vik, a blogger, wrote later, "but political fury, education, and rage."[64] It is framed by comments from incarcerated activist Larry Hoover, a former gang leader who encouraged voter participation in an election year during which, thanks to Dole, the Geto Boys became part of the campaign. But Bushwick Bill suggested that the importance of voting was much larger than a beef with an individual candidate. "We keep getting the short end of the stick because, since we don't think the vote is important, we don't vote and [the wrong] people get into office and never take care of our agenda," Bill told the *Washington Post*. "We should be involved in the decision-making about our own lives, and not just sitting around being the living dead."[65]

The Resurrection wasn't always as sophisticated as the voting talk would seem. One track contains some nasty ideas about Japanese Americans, and another uses homophobic slurs against J. Edgar Hoover. But the album offered the Geto Boys' response to continued criticism of gangsta rap and their attempt to move beyond its standard tropes. "I was watching movies like 'Do the Right Thing' and 'School Daze,' where at the end (actor) Laurence Fishburne yells 'Wake up!' and it really had an effect on me," Bushwick Bill told Greg Kot. "I realized we're all walking around asleep, intellectually comatose, dead to the facts. We were doing albums about big-booty women, drinking 40s, smoking weed and driving fancy cars and I realized we as a people still haven't gone beyond that."[66]

Vibe's Tracii McGregor recognized this shift, writing, "*The Resurrection* is a candid look at mobbing, at brothers and sisters not having the bare necessities, at the unemployment situation in Houston and across the country, at race relations between blacks and southern whites." Noting the album's "Wrath, gloom, desperation, power, evil," she evocatively declared that "*The Resurrection* is the real Song of the South."[67] Beyond the reference to Disney's racist fantasia, McGregor's words signaled the album's connection to a new wave of southern rappers, including Goodie Mob, OutKast, and 8 Ball & MJG, who built on the breakthroughs of first-wave artists such as the Geto Boys to create region-specific reckonings with the era's past and present. Musically, too, *The Resurrection* reflected the deepening of a soundscape specific to the South, with blues, soul, and even gospel textures moving to the forefront.

Bushwick Bill again delivered many of the album's most potent political rhymes, especially on two songs that use soul music as backing for their brooding meditations. "The World Is a Ghetto" remixes War's original by linking the deaths of people in Africa to police brutality and misconduct in Texas. Invoking Rwandan genocide, Bill says that white Americans treat Black and Brown folks in the ghetto just as badly, and that living conditions in the ghetto are so bad that refugees who come to the United States "see the same bullshit and head right back." "Geto Fantasy," meanwhile, imagines an alternate reality where the structural inequities and personal struggles might not be so hard. Bill delivers his verse with an unprecedented tenderness: "They want to see us stuck. Can't nobody ever say I didn't try to give a fuck. 'Cause I did and I do—the rest is up to you."

But after delivering this reassuring and hopeful message, he explodes into a discussion of his own pain on the next song, "I Just Wanna Die." This track takes an unflinching look at the effects of depression, opening with Bill asking if anyone can "stop the pain" and ending with the sound of a gunshot. The presence of "I Just Wanna Die" signaled a crucial element in Bushwick Bill's art that emerged in the 1990s alongside his focus on politics. As he became the public voice of the Geto Boys in battles against Republican presidential candidates and civil rights activists, he also publicly struggled with mental illness and drug addiction. Particularly after the self-inflicted gunshot wound that resulted in the loss of his eye in 1991, Bill made these conditions central to his music. By doing so, he reached a new level of creative depth and seized control of his story as others, including his bandmates, misrepresented or exploited it.

"HE AIN'T WHAT YOU EXPECT"

On June 20, 1991, drunk on Everclear and high on PCP, a depressed and delusional Richard Shaw tried to get his girlfriend to end his life.[1] He fought with her, and even threatened their infant child, before producing a gun that he tried to force into her hand and against his head. At some point, the gun went off and entered Shaw's skull through his right eye. He underwent emergency surgery to save his life. After a tenuous few hours, which included Shaw being pronounced dead, doctors successfully removed the bullet from his skull and he was stabilized. His wore a glass eye (sometimes accompanied by a patch) for the rest of his life.

While the reasons for his breakdown are not entirely clear, Shaw had previously struggled with depression, which had been exacerbated by the pressures of being a public figure and intensified by drug-fueled hallucinations. This incident occurred just after the Geto Boys finished recording *We Can't Be Stopped*. "On that album, we left no stone unturned lyrically," Bill remembered later. "We were talking about shit that no one else would."[2] This included not just politics but also themes of depression and paranoia, most notably on "Mind Playing Tricks on Me," which became their biggest single (No. 1 rap, No. 10 R&B) and most acclaimed track. With recording finished, all that remained was to shoot a cover to match the album's intensity and the group's notoriety. And then the phone call came from a Houston hospital.

Willie D couldn't remember who introduced the idea, "but somebody said: 'Shit, let's go down to the damn hospital and shoot it there.'"[3] Scarface suggested that James Prince was responsible for the decision: "He knew it was one of those images that would make you stop what you were doing as soon as you saw it and take a closer look like, What the fuck?"[4] They unhooked Shaw from his IV, removed the protective gauze from his face, and pushed his bed into a hallway. There, Scarface posed on one side and Willie D on the other, and Bushwick Bill sat between them with a defiant hand up and a cell phone propped up next to his ear. "People thought it was some artwork thing," Willie D recalled, "but that was the real deal."[5] This shocking image became central to the promotion of the album and remains an infamous cornerstone of the group's legend. "It was our way of saying, 'Yes, this really happened, America,'" remembered James Prince. "Deal with it."[6]

The man in the center of the photograph wasn't so sure. Shaw later expressed discomfort with how his damaged body and troubled psyche were paraded in front of the camera.[7] "It still hurts me to look at that cover because that was a personal thing I went through," he told Brian Coleman. "I really didn't understand why that picture was so important for them, important enough to take the IV out of my arm and endanger my life by taking the patch off my eye."[8] He criticized the group for exploiting his "tragedy" for the sake of commercial gain.[9] It led even his own family to see him as a monster: "I had family members that saw the album cover, nieces and nephews saw my eye, that would just scream and be like 'Oh, it's Uncle Billy, get him away from me!'"[10]

The photo for *We Can't Be Stopped* is very different from the Geto Boys' earlier covers. *Making Trouble* and *Grip It!* featured images that did not hide Bill's shortness but instead presented him standing alongside his bandmates in group shots that are wide enough to account for the height difference.[11] *Geto Boys* strayed from this pattern by featuring individual mugshots of each group member in a design that poked fun at the Beatles' *Let It Be*. Bill is the only one pictured shirtless, his muscled arms and chest exposed, but he's as poised as the other group members. On *We Can't Be Stopped*, Bill is grotesque, vulnerable, and in need of assistance.

These qualities mark the image as a potent demonstration of several historical representations of disabled people. The grotesquerie suggests the shocking display of authentic oddities during the height of freak shows. Bill's vulnerability as a hospital patient evokes the medicalization of disability, through which, as Rosemarie Garland-Thomson describes, "the wondrous monsters of antiquity, who became the fascinating freaks of the nineteenth century, transformed into the disabled people of the later twentieth century."[12] And Scarface and Willie D's participation in the photo suggests the complicated role of non-disabled allies whose desire to incorporate their disabled colleague could be outweighed by his value as a freakish gimmick. "When I sit back and look at it," Shaw recalled later, "Geto Boys was not getting the response from the audience until I came out dancing and doing everything I did, then everything changed." Bill noticed a similar dynamic in the album cover, which "would not have been interesting if they didn't come to the hospital and snap the picture without my permission."[13]

The promotion of *We Can't Be Stopped* and "Mind Playing Tricks on Me" strengthened this ambivalence. "All the interviewers were asking me was the reason I lost my eye because my mind was playing tricks on me," Bill recalled. His prominence in the Geto Boys, and the use of his physical difference as descriptor and metaphor in coverage of the group, took on a literally painful undertone. "I went out by myself a week after coming out the hospital, [and] for four months I was the only one promoting that record. Throwing up in every city, cuz I wasn't used to different climates and jet lag and all that shit and there was no medicine for the bacteria with my eye shit that I had to deal with and I'm just out there with my eye leaking and they said if it leaks into my other eye I could go blind and I'm doing all this shit for the record's sake."[14] Bushwick Bill had earned his spot as the group's most famous member, but it again seemed that people just wanted to stare at him.

Disabled people deal with this shit all the time. Even as we distinguish ourselves and gain friends or collaborators, we face the worry (if not the proof) that our presence and participation are motivated only by benign or malevolent expressions of ableism. We remain ready to be put on display, even by our friends, and we wonder if the attention we receive is because of our talents or because we are reconfirming some narrative of astonishing freaks or inspirational cripples. Bushwick Bill recognized that his contributions to the Geto Boys, from his dancing as Little Billy to his grotesque image on the cover of *We Can't Be Stopped*, could never be extricated from the novelty of his difference.

The 1991 shooting is the most often discussed moment in Bushwick Bill's life. It's covered in detail by Brian Coleman in an essay about *We Can't Be Stopped* (in his compendium of legendary hip-hop albums) and by Rolf Potts in his discussion of the earlier *Geto Boys* album. In her history of southern hip-hop, Tamara Palmer gives Bill "the lifetime achievement award for keeping it too real," saying that the album cover made him "one of America's first original reality stars."[15] Nearly every profile of and interview with Bill recounts the incident, starting immediately after it occurred. But very few of them consider the sadness or ambivalence that he expressed about the incident and its effects.

At the time, journalists attached "one-eyed" and similar phrases to their descriptions of Bill as a midget or dwarf. James Prince recalled that "politicians had a field day with that one: 'Here's another example of how the Geto Boys advocate senseless violence.'"[16] Activists campaigning against St. Ides malt liquor noted that the Geto Boys' endorsement of the product seemed particularly outrageous given that the shooting had been precipitated by alcohol.[17] And, as discussed earlier, it was used to explain Shaw's misogyny in the aftermath of the incident at the National Association of Black Journalists convention. Linda Stasi suggested that Bill's remarks justified "why his girlfriend shot his right eye out during a domestic dispute in 1991," and she was angered by the fact that "the 4-foot-6 Bill . . . actually used a picture from his 1991 eyeball shooting on his album."[18] As with his size, his new physical difference became additional and misunderstood shorthand for those who addressed the Geto Boys in this period.

As he did with his shortness, Bushwick Bill discussed the loss of his eye in his music. The shooting, as well as the mental illness that precipitated it, became a common theme for Bill in the Geto Boys and especially in the solo career he launched in 1992 with *Little Big Man*. He had addressed similar topics before, most infamously on "Mind of a Lunatic" and most powerfully on "Mind Playing Tricks on Me," but these themes gained new salience in the post-shooting recordings, in which Richard Shaw used his alter ego, Bushwick Bill, to examine new levels of autobiographical reflection. He exposed his wounds just as they had been uncovered on the infamous photo, except this time he was in control. As he raps on *Little Big Man*, "It's fucked up that I had to lose an eye to see shit clearly."

"Mind Playing Tricks on Me" presages this shift. Over a brooding Isaac Hayes sample, Scarface, Willie D, and Bushwick Bill describe being threatened by enemies who turn out to be hallucinations, a powerful counterpoint to the bluster that characterized gangsta and a piercing commentary on the fear that it created. "All of a sudden," Rodney Carmichael noted, "the villains depicted on record — and by society — were cast as the victims. They were haunted by their own demons, but also by the economic degradation that hollowed out the hoods from which they came."[19]

Bushwick's verse, which takes place on Halloween, follows him as he joins the Geto Boys on a devilish trick-or-treat mission where they're "robbin' little kids for cash." Written by Scarface, the lyrics find Bill fighting with a "six or seven feet" tall figure who is revealed to be a figment of his imagination. The image of Bill fighting with an enemy who exists only in his mind gains additional power through the height juxtaposition. "As a person with achondroplasia," Anna Hinton notes, "an extraordinarily tall person forces him to face the limitations that embodiment impose [*sic*]."[20] The size-specific image works even without Bill's dwarfism. In his memoir, Charlamagne Tha God relates to

Bill's fear of the tall man, saying it reminded him of the "boogeyman my parents would tell me to watch out for when I was a little kid."[21]

Charlamagne uses "Mind Playing Tricks on Me" to frame his memoir of living with anxiety, indicating the song's larger importance as one of the key early considerations of mental illness in hip-hop. "If you were black, if you felt the pressure of growing up with a target on your back, 'Mind Playing Tricks' was your anxiety anthem," Rodney Carmichael noted. "'Mind Playing Tricks' became the Trojan Horse, giving a generation the language to consider something we'd never let down our guard to talk about."[22] Such songs created a space for rap artists, particularly men, to relate their psychological travails not just as the products of a crazy-making world but as personal struggles that should be approached with care. These discussions of the "mind of a lunatic" were not the source of voyeuristic shock but instead a vehicle for empathy. References to mental illness, which became a main strain of commercial rap in the 2010s, can't be traced solely to "Mind Playing Tricks on Me." But the song played a key role in showing how rap artists could leverage "keep it real" honesty into heartfelt discussions of psychological disorders.

For Kiana Fitzgerald, Bushwick Bill's verse was particularly resonant. "My late mother suffered from depression and other undiagnosed mental health issues," she wrote following Bill's death, and "Mind Playing Tricks on Me" became her mother's "favorite song of all time," particularly Bill's verse, for which "she came alive" and "rapped along with the record."[23] Fitzgerald herself was later diagnosed with bipolar disorder and schizophrenia, and she took solace in the song after an episode caused her to move back to Houston. "Home is where I finally and fully appreciate the verses of Scarface and Willie D, but especially Bushwick Bill, whose presence on the track lit my mother's eyes up with joy, and later brought life back into my own."[24] Fitzgerald notes that beyond his comic abilities and talent for creating "tales of dark mischief," it was Bill's self-acceptance that made him so important to her and other listeners.

This dynamic of self-acceptance and the textured beauty of songs like "Mind Playing Tricks on Me" are ignored in even the most positive assessments of Bushwick Bill, but they became key to his work after the shooting. The braggadocio was still there, often through direct and indirect callbacks to "Size Ain't Shit," as were the twisted fantasies that gained new depth through Bill's "Chuckie" persona (more on him later). But these were now leavened and enriched by meditative tracks in which Bill described his depression and addiction, and how they were connected to his height and partial loss of vision. He avoided the self-pity of what he called "poor little me" songs, instead pairing his struggles with narratives of survival and some of the old trickster magic.

Bill mapped this new terrain on *Little Big Man*, the 1992 solo debut album that arrived less than a year after the shooting.[25] As Mikko Koivisto notes, the album "used many of the Geto Boys' stylistic and thematic strategies, such as graphic depictions of murder and sexual violence, but it also included more personal insights about his disabilities: dwarfism, depression and vision impairment."[26] The album's first single, "Ever So Clear," was a brooding retelling of the shooting and what led to it; despite its heavy content and lack of a hook, the song became his biggest solo hit. Bolstered by his Geto Boys fame and propelled by "Ever So Clear," *Little Big Man* became Bushwick Bill's highest-charting album on the *Billboard* 200 and his most satisfying solo effort. Shea Serrano called it one of the best Houston rap albums, saying it "represented the most honest, visceral effort of [Bill's] career."[27]

"Ever So Clear" was a turning point for Bill, as important as "Size Ain't Shit" or "Mind of a Lunatic" and a direct commentary on both. It opens with a verse that details Bill's feelings of always being an outcast and misfit because of his shortness. "I used to get funny looks 'cause I was small, and trying to make it was like running through a brick wall." He notes that his Geto Boys' notoriety made him "the spice around town" but didn't necessarily make it easier to fit in: "I got friends and bitches on my dick, but when they look at Richard all they see is Bushwick." (Given his feelings about *We Can't Be Stopped*, one wonders if the other Geto Boys were included in this category.) He directs particular ire at women who mistreated him, crossing the line from bluesy honesty into petty sexism, but also deflating the boasts of "Size Ain't Shit" by suggesting that the sexual attention he received from women was contingent on his fame and the novelty of being with a short person. The latter is a very recognizable concern for short folks since our height can make us interesting to strangers who want to talk with us, dance with us, or do other things.

The second verse of "Ever So Clear" merges "Mind of a Lunatic" and "Mind Playing Tricks on Me" by mixing the graphic storytelling of the former with the latter's deep blues. Turning his attention to the shooting, Bill acknowledges his guilt in attacking his girlfriend and describes the evening in gruesome detail. It's explicit but not gratuitous. The horror story continues in the third verse, with Bill fighting for life. He references the infamous photo— "With an IV in my arm, I took a picture for an album cover. Goddamn, this shit's a trip, G" — and notes that even as his family members prayed for his life, he still had "suicidal thoughts, hoping that I don't make it." But with God "steady urging me" to keep going, he came back. "I'm glad that I'm here, G, but it's fucked up I had to lose an eye to see shit clearly," he concludes, reframing the song's central pun and referencing the inner sight that now linked him to historical images of blind musicians of the past. Accompanied by an affecting video, "Ever So Clear" modeled how Bushwick Bill would use his notoriety to direct his audience toward a more serious consideration of his experiences.

Little Big Man contains the usual mix of sex, violence,

and politics, but its most notable tracks take this new approach. For one thing, as Mikko Koivisto points out, "the rapper describes numerous instances when he became an object of ridicule and abuse because of his height."[28] On the first track, "Intro," Bill connects this treatment to his larger critiques of American society for the first time. An unidentified voice insults his music and calls him un-American, to which Bill responds with his standard set of rejoinders. But then the insults turn more personal: "I feel sorry for you 'cause you're short." Bill responds by telling his story like a typical narrative of overcoming disability before taking a welcome trickster turn: "I was born short. But see what I did was I enabled myself, right, to obtain wisdom, knowledge and overstanding. So, mentally . . . I could reach things that you can't reach, because you can't even realize your own handicap. And I could see even clearer how to fuck over your bitch ass because of that shit." And then, just as he did at the beginning of "Size Ain't Shit," he laughs.

Bill makes a similar structural connection on the ruminative "Copper to Cash." Over a sample from The O'Jays' "For the Love Of Money," Bill relates the economic hardship he faced due to the combined effects of his Blackness and his size. "Everything'd be fine if I was working 9 to 5," he laments, "But I can't get that kinda job, I ain't 5 feet high." (This is an accurate representation of continuing employment discrimination against disabled people.) He suggests that his inability to find work because of his dwarfism pushed him toward a life of illegal activity, and he then evocatively notes that "they don't realize that my size ain't shit."

Not everything on *Little Big Man* is as ruminative as these tracks, but Bill includes references to his height in the sex jokes and violent threats. The title track works its oxymoron into a discussion of Bill's power and prowess, complete with Jamaican patois. He pulls a similar move on "Don't Come Too Big" and "Call Me Crazy," which opens with Bill shooting a man who's making fun of his height. Throughout, and in whatever mode, *Little Big Man* is easily the most extensive discussion of shortness in pop history, with size being a central element to Bill's broader reclamation of his story. As he raps at one point, "Bushwick is back, and I ain't what you expect."

Bill explored this territory further on his 1995 album, *Phantom of the Rapra*. Beyond the Bob Dole–dissing politics discussed earlier, it contains the bluesy "Whatcha Gonna Do" and "Times Is Hard," which link his personal struggles to those facing everyone else in the world. And he confronts his suicidal ideations on "Only God Knows," where Bill lays bare his emotions. "I'm in so much pain it hurts my heart to wake up," he admits. "Stress is eatin' and my mind is playin' tricks again. It's tellin' me that I ain't shit, it's tellin' me to quit."

Suicide appeared again on the Geto Boys' 1996 album, *The Resurrection*, with "I Just Wanna Die."[29] This song is another very difficult listen, pairing Bill's reflections with a bracing sound and guttural delivery. It opens with Bill shouting, "What can we do with all this fucking pain? Somebody stop the pain!"—a literal cry for help. He insists that listeners contend with these struggles as much as they would with the more outlandish elements of the group's catalog. "I wanna bring you smooth into my nightmare," he offers. "Don't be afraid of watching life bleed. Explore my every thought, come out and sightsee." At the end the group dramatizes Bill ending his life with a gunshot as Willie D expresses first skepticism and then horror at Bill's actions.

We should not assume that Bill is relating the contents of his mind here. Just as too many critics of the period assumed that the Geto Boys (and other rap artists) were simply reporting their experiences rather than crafting narratives, it would be a mistake to assume that these painful stories were straight confession rather than creative choices. But to whatever degree they were fictional or autobiographical, Bushwick Bill insisted that audiences address this less sensational aspect of what might go on in the "Mind of a Lunatic" and the body of "Size Ain't Shit." He did so while mostly avoiding judgment or pathology, presenting depression as neither shameful nor hopeless.

Bill further destigmatized depression and suicidal ideation by connecting them to shortness. Rebecca Cokley, in a 2017 discussion of the problem of suicide among people with dwarfism, said, "I don't think that a majority of my community are depressed because they're little people, however I have no doubt that society's objectification of little people adds insult to injury (literally) and can push folks over the edge."[30] Cokley lists as reasons for these feelings everything from personal isolation to employment discrimination to the mockery of little people in photos and videos by abled people. All of these had been mentioned specifically by Bushwick Bill in his lyrics and in interviews as contributing factors to the fragility of his mental health. After the 1991 shooting, Bill insisted that his differences would be fodder not just for laughs or scares but also for serious meditations on pain and perseverance.

Of course, he wasn't giving up on laughs or scares. Tarbox Kiersted remembers attending a Rap-a-Lot event in Houston where he noticed that Bill's unpatched eye didn't look right: it "veered around, spookily. It unnerved me." Noting Kiersted's confusion, Bill "leaned in conspiratorially and, smiling like a maniac, flipped up his eyepatch. It was covering his good eye, not the bad one." Laughing, Bill told Kiersted that he rigged a small hole in his patch so that he could see while using his bad eye to scare people. When Kiersted asked why, Bill replied, "Gotta always keep 'em guessing."[31]

Although "Ever So Clear" and other tracks signaled a new side to Bushwick Bill, he was still up to his old tricks. Back on *We Can't Be Stopped*, he introduced a new persona that gave potency to his signature mix of horror and humor, and further signified on stereotypes surrounding short-statured people. But in keeping with his new approach, he also used this alter ego to further dramatize his internal struggles. Just as he had gotten personal and political in the 1990s, Bill opened a third artistic lane that propelled his work and increased his influence. Let's head back to 1991. It's time to meet Chuckie.

CHILD'S PLAY

On the fifth track of *We Can't Be Stopped*, over creepy-crawling rhythm, Bushwick Bill introduced the character of Chuckie in a song based on the horror villain of the same name from the *Child's Play* movies. Released in 1988, the first *Child's Play* centered on the murderous activities of Chuckie, an adorable doll who becomes possessed by the spirit of a serial murderer. A campy mix of violence and humor, *Child's Play* became a breakout hit, launched a long-running franchise, and made its unlikely villain into a household name.

Written by Houston's Gangsta N-I-P, the song "Chuckie" finds Bill rapping about horrifying acts of violence and using the character to symbolize his divided mental state: "Half my body is Chuckie, the other half is Bushwick." The two characters then battle and collaborate over an unsettling track where Bill uses a lower voice than usual. "Chuckie" is as bracing an introduction as "Size Ain't Shit," and he makes sure you get the connection. "I told you size wasn't shit, that's why I murdered your nieces," the song opens. "Wasn't my fault they found they head cut in 88 pieces." And, as usual, he laughs, although this time it's the doll's playful giggle, which then transforms into the yelps of a murderous monster.

Bushwick Bill adopted Chuckie as an alter ego for the rest of his career. He included Chuckie through reappearances or references on every subsequent album, usually in songs that involved discussions of psychological turmoil. He carried a Chuckie doll on stage and in press appearances for several years and even merged their names on later albums, rapping as Chuckwick and using the distinctive voice he had introduced in the first Chuckie song. The voice wasn't an impression of the movie character, who spoke in a nasal whine, but the lower register suggested that when Chuckie came out, we were slipping even further into Bushwick Bill's nightmare.

Chuckie gave Bill another connection to horror cinema, which he cited as both an influence and defense. He often compared his lyrics to Freddy Krueger, Jason, and other scary-movie characters, not to mention real-life horror shows such as the Manson Family and US foreign policy. Beyond this, Bill noted the influence of directors from Brian De Palma to Spike Lee to Michael Moore. In 1990 Bill said, "When Alfred Hitchcock directed *Psycho* he filmed from a maniac's point of view — his fears, his feelings, his thoughts. That's how we wrote 'Mind of a Lunatic.'"[1] Just as with Brad Jordan's adoption of the character Scarface, Bill's use of Chuckie contextualized the Geto Boys' music and reminded critics that their (racist) assumptions were incorrect.

The incorporation of horror culture with gangsta rap structured a new hip-hop subgenre, horrorcore, for which the Geto Boys were key originators. At its best, horrorcore amplifies the drama of rap's narratives by deploying horror's cinematic language and doomy sonic atmosphere.[2] "The supernatural offers rappers a new world of hard gore in which to set their boasts, threats and tales," Neil Strauss wrote in 1994 in an early assessment of the trend. "Talking about death can also be a good way of putting life in perspective."[3]

The South was particularly fertile ground for horrorcore. The region's blues traditions — with images of devils, demons, and hauntings — offered precedents and signifiers, as did the linked tradition of southern gothic literature. "If these guys had little else in common with William Faulkner and Flannery O'Connor," Roni Sarig noted of the Geto Boys, "they were at least firmly in a territory that Dixie artists had cultivated for generations."[4] The doomy textures of horrorcore were well suited to artists from Houston, Memphis, and other southern cities because this subgenre of hip-hop mixed the South's fantastical traditions with gritty depictions of the political and economic aftermath of the civil rights movement and white backlash.[5]

While not the only progenitors of horrorcore, the Geto Boys influenced the work of horror rappers from the Memphis group Three 6 Mafia to Eminem. "Chuckie" is one of several Geto Boys tracks noted as key horrorcore texts. Its writer, Ganksta N-I-P, has been called horrorcore's inventor thanks to the bloodcurdling recordings he started making in Houston in the late 1980s, and he was hired specifically to craft a new persona for Bushwick Bill.[6] Bill's verses on "Mind of a Lunatic" and "Mind Playing Tricks on Me" have also been noted as templates due to their outrageousness and their references to movie characters, but "Chuckie" made the firmest and fullest connection between Bushwick Bill, the horror movies he loved, and the horrorcore hip-hop that he was helping to popularize.

Bill's specific affinity with Chuckie went deeper than his horror fandom, of course. As he told David Mills in 1991, "I kept watching all the different 'Child's Play' sagas, right? Then all of a sudden I decided, 'He's short, I'm short. What a better concept?'"[7] Bill recognized Chuckie as another short figure assumed to be harmless but out to cause chaos. Subverting the jolly elves, helpful Munchkins, and seven dwarfs of cinema's past, Chuckie, like Bushwick Bill, defies the perception that short people are adorable curiosities. But again, like Bill, he also embodies fears about the danger represented by short people through their violation of physical and social norms.[8]

Like so much of the Geto Boys' music, the *Child's Play* series is based on shattering white fantasies of safety. In the first film, Chuckie launches his reign of terror by manipulating the expectations of a so-called normal family, white and middle-class, called the Barclays, who buy the cute doll for their children.[9] The consumerist fable becomes a literal nightmare as Chuckie, possessed by the spirit of a serial killer in a voodoo ritual, awakens to go on a murderous rampage. As he kills, he mocks his victims with a mischievous smirk. In both word and deed, Chuckie was the little devil who nobody saw coming—a perfect avatar for Bushwick Bill. "Like Chuckie," Anna Hinton notes, "he is small yet horrifically violent and invincible."[10]

The song "Chuckie" builds this connection through both sound and lyrics. The track, which Kiana Fitzgerald describes as "skin-prickling," is based around samples from the movie and blends gross-out imagery (at one point, Bill/Chuckie describes "eating a dog's brain") with real-life dangers such as crack addiction and the Iraq War.[11] The song makes unsurprising use of the imagery of childhood. The hook signifies on the source material by declaring that killing is just "child's play," and Bill/Chuckie follows a boast of "I might be small but my nuts are big" with the warning that "The worst that you could do is let me keep your fuckin' kids."

This imagery wasn't new. Dwarf characters had long been used in folklore to destabilize what Lori Merish calls "the conventional boundary between child and adult."[12] As far back as the devious Rumpelstiltskin, who steals the first child of the heroine, short people were presented as trolls or tricksters who subverted domestic norms. Horror films repeated this trope, sometimes without any context. In the 1971 movie *Don't Look Now*, Donald Sutherland's protagonist pursues a woman he believes is his deceased daughter through the streets of Venice, only to find out the figure is a murderous dwarf who in the movie's shock ending fatally knifes Sutherland's character. The 2009 movie *Orphan* concerns a family that adopts a nine-year-old girl before realizing that she is actually a thirty-three-year-old with stunted growth who murdered her previous families. She also tries to seduce her new adopted father. All of the *Child's Play* movies worked this territory, including *Bride of Chucky* (1998), which offered a horror/camp remix of the fascination with dwarf marriage that went back to the Barnum-promoted wedding of Tom Thumb and Lavinia Warren.

This is only one example of the wider use of disabled characters as monsters in cinema. The term *monster* itself has roots in understandings of physical difference, and it was once used to describe people who would later be rebranded as freaks and, eventually, disabled.[13] As suggested by this origin, a monster is meant to inspire a mix of emotions, including curiosity and terror but also wonder and pity due to their distance from normality.[14] In Hollywood, freakish bodies—the hairy Wolfman, Frankenstein's gigantic creature, the mutated lead character of *The Fly*—propelled the horror genre as it explored terrible, unsettling, and sometimes sympathetic monsters who longed to fit in even as they wreaked havoc.

The most influential example is *Freaks*, the Tod Browning film that was released in 1931 but remains a controversial horror touchstone and a foundational text in cinematic depictions of the disabled. Part subversive satire and part crude corrective, *Freaks* presents a group of sideshow performers who exact revenge on a villainous able-bodied singer named Cleopatra after she false-heartedly seduces Hans, a performer with dwarfism. She pretends to love him and tries to convince him to dump his lover Freida (also short), all in an attempt to kill him and gain access to his fortune. Cleopatra disdains the freaks' physicality and mocks their community, laughing at their ritual shouting of "One of us! One of us!" when a new oddity joins the troupe. When Hans discovers the plot, he leads the freaks as they terrorize Cleopatra before turning her into a grotesque human-duck hybrid. At the end of the film, Hans enjoys his riches while rekindling his romance with Freida. And, just like Bushwick Bill and Chuckie, he laughs.

Like *Child's Play*, the drama of *Freaks* stems from the perception of dwarfs and otherwise disabled characters as childlike and thus not dangerous.[15] As Joan Hawkins notes, "The entire revenge sequence can be read as a systematic reversal of [an earlier scene that] attempted to establish the freaks as harmless children."[16] She also suggests that the film's implication of earlier "freak violence" further disputes the childlike associations and suggests that a more sinister impulse lurks beneath.[17] Even the movie's slogan — "Can a full grown woman truly love a midget?" — revealed the disruption of domestic norms symbolized by its short antihero.

Chuckie, though, is not a person with dwarfism; he's not even human. But the anthropomorphized doll, a literal plaything, holds the same narrative power. Most of all, Chuckie (like Bushwick Bill) runs a knife through one of the most destructive stereotypes attached to short people. Simply put, people think we're cute.

The association of cuteness with short people—the unending "aww"—shapes our experiences in innumerable frustrating ways. It justifies invasions of our physical space and assumptions about our personal lives, and it frames too many of our social interactions. As Lori Merish explains, the labeling of short people as cute is a form of social policing that "aestheticizes" and regulates "the (shifting) boundaries between Selves and Others" or "'humans' and 'freaks.'"[18] Cuteness offers tall people a framework to understand and theoretically identify with us, but it also prevents us from being considered fully adult.[19] As Merish notes, short people "could be drawn into the cute's structure of maternal proprietorship and 'protection'" while remaining objects that regular-sized people can coo over and play with. She points out that "Domesticating the Otherness of little people entailed a curtailment of desire, especially sexual desire."[20] In other words, we become child's play. This happens all the time. And it fucking sucks.

Chuckie gave Bushwick Bill his best opportunity to critique this misperception, but he also satirized it in his appearance in 1993 on the popular sitcom *Martin*. He played Tre, the leader of a violent gang of "little people" who beat up Martin's friend Tommy for stealing Tre's girlfriend. Later they threaten the whole crew in an alley, where Tommy delivers a speech that doubles as both a heartfelt call for peace and a parody of the Stop the Violence tropes common in Black pop culture of the period. After initial skepticism, Tre says, "That's the first time anybody ever broke it down to me like that." He pauses, looking emotional, and then goes in for a hug. "Aw, homie," he admits, "my mind's playing tricks on me." The crowd roars its approval.

The humor of the episode resides in the notion that short people could never pose a threat to the full-sized.[21] When Martin and company talk with police after being ambushed by Tre's gang, the officer asks, "Where were their parents?" and laughs, as does the audience. Their attacks parody gangland violence parables and echo the climax of *Freaks*. Also, from the episode's focus on Tre's love life to the repeated jokes about Tre leering at Martin's girlfriend, Gina, the show drew laughs at the idea of a little person posing a sexual threat as well. By gaining advantage over Martin's taller men, Tre was a comical version of Bushwick Bill's larger project of demonstrating that treating little people like a child's plaything would not end well.

Successful movies often lead to sequels, and Bill understood cinematic storytelling well enough to bring Chuckie back on his 1992 solo album, *Little Big Man*. In one track he declares, "It's the replay of 'Chuckie,' part 2, call it 'Chuckwick,'" and the song even contains a long sample from its inspiration's second chapter, *Child's Play 2.* Like any good follow-up, "Chuckwick" is partly a retread (he repeats the "Size Ain't Shit" reference almost verbatim) and partly an escalation of the original's themes and imagery. Bill describes himself as an "insane-ass dwarf" and "the world's smallest killer" while he goes even further into the character's evil mystery. "Sometimes I'm invisible, sometimes I'm seen," he says. "Sometimes I'm a pitchfork, sometimes I'm guillotine." But just in case you get too scared, he opens with a sampled ad for a "collection of ghoulish sounds" that can "make your own sound terrifying and terrible," reminding us that it's all just a performance.

"Chuckwick" is the last song that Bushwick Bill devoted entirely to exploring the Chuckie persona, perhaps because he recognized that more songs would yield the same diminishing returns as the movie sequels. But the character haunted subsequent albums. Bill drops the name "Chuck" or "Chuckwick" in reference to his murderous or sexual exploits, even introducing the romantic "Chuck Nice" at one point. But he also symbolizes the life Bill was trying to leave behind. On his 2001 track "That's Life," he worries that unspecified "people" are "pushing Bushwick into Chuckie" even as he tries to stay focused. When he embraced gospel on the album *My Testimony of Redemption* (2009), Bill said that when he decided to leave secular music, he "traded Chuckwick into being a Jesus Freak." As he told *Texas Monthly* in 2013, "Once I took on the persona of Chucky, I just became this short person that wasn't afraid to die and was scared to live."[22]

Signaling this slippage, Chuckwick and the lowered voice used to perform the character show up on some of Bill's most unsettling material. *Little Big Man*'s druggy "Skitso," for example, pairs slasher fantasies (including lyrics from "Mind of a Lunatic") with spoken interludes from an unidentified voice telling Bill that he's "here to get you out" if he would just tell the doctor he's feeling better. Instead, Bill/Chuckwick doubles down on the violence, eventually scaring both the doctor and his friend away. Any sense of horror-show fun that existed in "Mind of a Lunatic" is undercut by spoken interludes and an arrangement that includes screams over the top of skittering synths. With Chuckwick in control, "Skitso" is a Geto Boys remix that is literally and figuratively located inside an insane asylum.

Bill uses Chuckie to similarly compelling effect on two tracks from the 1995 album *Phantom of the Rapra*. "Already Dead" is legitimately disturbing; like "Skitso," it is distinguished by wailing sounds in the background. This effect frames a lyric that finds Bill returning to the vulnerability he feels because of his multiple disabilities:

Look into my eyes
Or should I say my eye
And, nigga, you see just why

This cat afraid to die
Ever since birth I've been givin' the short hand
It didn't hurt but it made me a smart man.

But on the hard-driving "Subliminal Criminal," he flips the script, rapping that Chuckwick is "the Fifth Ward hard crippler." Throughout these later appearances Chuckwick is both threatening and threatened, representing an internal battle that Bushwick Bill codes specifically to his mental and physical condition.

Even beyond Chuckie's appearances, *Phantom of the Rapra* engages the horror tradition thanks to Bill's adoption of the titular character. Created by French novelist Gaston Leroux in 1911, *The Phantom of the Opera* is another story of bodily freakishness, with the character's disfigurement symbolizing his alienation from a society that perceives him as dangerous. He is marked different both by his disfigured face, which is revealed by Lon Chaney in a famous moment of early horror cinema, and by the mask he wears to hide his true self. Thanks to the success of the Broadway musical in the 1980s and early 1990s, the Phantom was enjoying perhaps his greatest moment of cultural resonance at the time of Bill's remix of the character. He drew connections between the two musical styles, stating that "rap is opera to people in the ghetto," insisting on links that audiences might not have considered.[23]

The Phantom of the Rapra uses this potent allusion to animate its discussions of otherness. The cover finds him at a piano at the bottom of a staircase, with the Phantom's mask hanging over his head, implying that he is both aware of the disguise and unwilling to put it on. Bill frames the album with spoken tracks that suggest how the character symbolizes the misunderstandings about hip-hop and Bill himself. He links the Phantom's disguise to both the Black cultural practice of masking and people's attempts to hide their evil intentions behind a comforting facade. At the very end he warns against trusting a racist United States: over mournful piano, he says that "it's like they all wear a mask. . . . Illusion is the ultimate weapon." While not as sustained as his engagement with Chuckie, Bill's use of the Phantom of the Opera, a tragic character whose physical difference causes him to be misunderstood and hated by those who love his music but fear the artist behind it, is just as poignant a connection.

Chuckwick makes a few appearances on Bill's later solo albums. Most of these, such as "Tragedy" (2001) and "Willbushwick" (2005), use the split vocal timbre to reflect on the real-life horrors of personal and societal turmoil. "Tragedy" blames a demon for ills ranging from AIDS to the crack epidemic, while "Willbushwick" talks about imprisonment and police harassment as exacerbating factors contributing to mental illness. There's also "20Minutsormore (Chuckwick Version)," which remixes the playful come-on of the album's single into something both more threatening and more erotic. The returns of Chuckie feel like new chapters rather than hard reboots, forming a sustained narrative that paralleled Bill's repetition of imagery from "Size Ain't Shit" and "Ever So Clear."

By the late 1990s, Bill's Chuckie persona had helped inspire a new generation of horrorcore rappers who built on the early innovations of the Geto Boys, Ganksta N-I-P, and others to create new nightmares for a growing and diversifying audience. Artists such as Gravediggaz (from New York) and Bone-Thugz-N-Harmony (from Cleveland) scored crossover hits with music that drew from horrorcore's roots. In Memphis, horrorcore became a particularly important component of the city's rap scene, with Three 6 Mafia emerging as the most prominent of the horror-influenced artists who have defined the city's signature sound from the 1990s to the present.[24] As Roni Sarig notes, the Memphis crew bore a specific resemblance to the Geto Boys, thanks to the "shadowy persona" and "shriveled arm" of co-founder DJ Paul; "like Bushwick Bill," Sarig suggests, DJ Paul "seemed ripped from the pages of some urbanized Southern gothic novel."[25] Beyond this, Three 6 Mafia sampled the Geto Boys and spoke of them as an influence as they put Memphis on the map.

The Detroit-based horrorcore artists Insane Clown Posse, whose adoption of clown makeup worked its own juxtaposition of childishness and danger, were also enthusiastic fans of the group. The white rappers built a large cult following throughout the 1990s and included a cover of "Assassins" on their highest-charting album.[26] Bushwick Bill performed solo at an early incarnation of the group's annual Gathering of the Juggalos and joined the Geto Boys for their performance at the festival in 2012. The Geto Boys performed again at the 2019 event, which took place two months after Bill's death. At one point, Scarface called for a moment of silence in honor of their fallen bandmate, and the crowd, which had been setting off firecrackers, stood in comparative silence with their fists raised in tribute.[27]

Another white horrorcore rapper from Detroit became hip-hop's most successful artist at the turn of the millennium. Eminem broke through in the late 1990s with an outrageous style that blended violence, sex, humor, and psychological conflict in a manner that bore the clear influence of the Geto Boys. Eminem acknowledged the specific impact of Bushwick Bill, calling him a "pioneering legend" and "one-of-a-kind MC" in a tweet after Bill's death, and paying musical tribute on his 2020 track "Little Engines."[28] The song appears on *Music to Get Murdered By*, an album that foregrounds the nightmarish vibes in Eminem's work and opens with a sample from Alfred Hitchcock, who also inspired Bill. On "Little Engines," Eminem shouts out Bill in a brief lyric, part of a track that, from its opening Hitchcock clip to its "Mind of a Lunatic"–style riff on Charles Manson, reflects the language that Bushwick Bill deployed so effectively. (Even the "heigh-ho!" reference that follows the Bill name-drop could be interpreted as an acknowledgment of how he challenged cinematic representations of dwarfs. Or maybe it's just a cheap joke. Or maybe both.) Beyond the horror touchstones, the ongoing battle between Slim Shady and Marshall Mathers for control of Eminem's psyche (a central motif on his records) bears clear resemblance to the relationship between Bushwick Bill and Chuckie.

In 2005 an interviewer for "HoustonSoReal" noted this similarity, and Bushwick Bill didn't mince words. He called Eminem a "sell-out" who had "taken black music and [is] making more money than the average black artist. What Eminem is doing is what Elvis did to Little Richard." He also complained that Eminem didn't rap about "white issues" and crimes like "credit-card scams" or "bank fraud."[29] While perhaps an oversimplification of Eminem's work, Bill's comments fit his longer argument that real horrors exist because of systemic injustice, and he expressed justifiable concern about how the biggest-selling rapper of the moment was appropriating the innovations of Black artists such as the Geto Boys.

Eminem's influence, or at least the desire to counter his appropriation, is evident on "Dirty Bitch," a Bill-led track from the Geto Boys' 2005 reunion album, *The Foundation*. Released around the same time as Bill's "HoustonSoReal" interview, "Dirty Bitch" reflects the album's reinvigoration of the classic Geto Boys approach by bridging horrorcore outrage with emotional vulnerability. In a spoken intro, Bill details a failed love affair that drove him to violence against a woman who calls him "short" and "ugly." In its mix of sadness and anger (and sexism), with shortness foregrounded and mental stability questioned, "Dirty Bitch" is a fitting demonstration of Bill's key tropes. With a skittering sound that recalls Dr. Dre's productions for Eminem, and a brutally misogynist lyric, it was hard not to hear Slim Shady lurking in the shadows. Or maybe it was Chuckie.

By the time Bill recorded "Dirty Bitch," he had gone through some difficult years. He left the Geto Boys in the late 1990s. His solo career, after the success of *Little Big Man* and *Phantom of the Rapra*, had sputtered both creatively and commercially. And he continued to struggle with drug and alcohol issues that exacerbated his mental health problems and led to run-ins with the law. In the new century, though, Bill adopted a surprising role as an elder statesman. He reteamed with the Geto Boys for *The Foundation*, mentored younger artists (including his son), and released a solo album that seemed like a shocking departure but actually reflected the roots of his artistry and the long journey he had taken since then.

"BRAND NEW PREACHER, RAP GAME TEACHER"

In 2005, just before the release of the Geto Boys' comeback album *The Foundation*, a Houston-based blogger named Matt Sonzala asked Bushwick Bill where he'd been.[1] It was a fair question. Bill left the Geto Boys in the late 1990s, and the group had been largely inactive even as they grew in reputation as forefathers of Houston rap and the Dirty South movement that had become central to hip-hop by the turn of the millennium. Scarface had launched an acclaimed solo career that built on the Geto Boys' revered recordings, and Willie D had released his own successful solo albums on Rap-a-Lot. But Bill's albums, which were released independently, floundered. A dwindling audience greeted releases that, as Shea Serrano noted, "felt either a little too forced . . . or a lot too aimless" as they revisited Bushwick's well-worn themes over clear and sometimes awkward responses to new musical trends.[2]

Even though they're largely ignored in appreciations of Bushwick Bill's life and career, there are moments on *No Surrender, No Retreat* (1998), *Universal Small Soujlah* (2001), and *Gutta Mix* (2005) that stand with the best of his solo work. "Stand By Me" and "20minutsormore" offer memorable remixes of the "Size Ain't Shit" brags. "Unforgiven" blends blues desperation with a gospel-infused call for rescue. And "Farenheit9one1" — another movie reference, this time to a Michael Moore documentary — is one of Bill's most memorable polemics, juxtaposing 9/11-themed lyrics with spoken segments about the dangers of being Black in Los Angeles. The voiceovers and rapping intrude on each other, which makes for a jarring listen that communicates the song's message more effectively than any of Bill's lyrics, even his insistent cries of "You have the right to vote!" at the end. With humor, anger, and vulnerability, the best songs on Bill's later albums remind listeners of earlier highlights.

Despite these highlights, there is no way to miss the decline. Bill's core tropes — the Chuckie routines, "Mind of a Lunatic" posturing, "Size Ain't Shit" lewdness, and "Ever So Clear" meditations — feel increasingly clichéd on these records, especially when paired with listless arrangements that lack the spark of earlier releases. Lyrics and even entire songs appear on multiple albums without alteration. And, most notably, numerous tracks find Bill appearing only briefly (popping in for a spoken intro or to help deliver the hook) or not at all in favor of ceding the floor to guest artists.

The dormancy of Bill's solo career paralleled continued personal problems. His battles with addiction led to further hospitalizations and arrests, and his personal relationships remained tumultuous. In 2000 he was arrested for domestic violence and arson after his girlfriend's house burned to the ground; news clips from the incident opened 2001's *Universal Small Souljah*.[3] Despite growing respect for the Geto Boys as godfathers of the Dirty South, Bushwick Bill's rare appearances in the public eye were either in recollection of past glories or in light of present problems.

Both were implied by his response to the question posed to him in 2005 about his recent whereabouts. Bill mentioned his continuing releases, but he seemed more interested in a different project. "I been making money helping people set up record labels," he said. "Getting publishing companies started and having everything copywritten and licensed and all that. That's what I make my money from. Helping people that's local in certain cities that got talent but just don't know how to coordinate with other people to get their music nationwide."[4] This may have been bluster or hype, but it signaled a turning point in Bill's work and cultural presence in the twenty-first century. During this period Bill crafted both public and private roles as a teacher, using his experiences and the esteem for the Geto Boys to reach a new generation of artists and audiences.

Most who have told the story of Bushwick Bill stop in the mid-1990s; even the posthumous tributes skip over the last twenty years of his life before addressing his cancer as a sad end for a once great artist. If any of Bill's activities in the last two decades of his life get mentioned, it's usually briefly and sometimes mockingly. But Bushwick Bill had not disappeared. He rejoined the Geto Boys for one of their best albums; he battled personal issues while embracing his role as a father and mentor to his son, the aspiring rapper Yung KNXW; and in 2009 he released *My Testimony of Redemption*, a return to form that represents both a summation of his career and a potential way forward. His announcement of his illness in 2019 and the remembrances that followed his death possessed a depth that would have surprised many of his staunchest haters and maybe even some of his biggest fans. Bill never got old, but he did age gracefully for a while.

Bushwick Bill's reunion with Scarface and Willie D for the 2005 album *The Foundation* was a stunning artistic return for the Geto Boys. Looking back on a rap landscape that they helped create, they asserted their continued relevance while taking stock as they entered their third decade. Maybe it was the encouragement of his old collaborators, or maybe it was the fact that he didn't need to carry an entire album, but Bill's contributions to *The Foundation* were his best in a decade. He contributes his usual shout-outs to Chuckwick violence and "Size Ain't Shit" tricksterism. He relates his escapades as the "little motherfucker with the big dick swingin'," ranging from the boasts of "We Boogie" to the horrors of "Dirty Bitch." He rails against crooked cops and economic injustice, and even finds time for Jamaican-style toasting on "Yes, Yes, Y'all," where he refers to himself as "Little Richard, like the singer." And the reflective storyteller returns on the album's two most emotionally resonant tracks.

"I Tried" is a confession of sins over a warm soul track. On his verse, Bill brings the story of "Ever So Clear" to the Geto Boys, lamenting the difficulties he'd faced over the years. Referencing the hypervisibility created by both his fame and his stature, he notes that he tried to escape and "change my name for anonymity's sake," but "a four feet dwarf that be on television's hard to miss." He also laments that his legal troubles and personal challenges caused him to be separated from his children as he struggled, but he expresses hope that they know he'll be around for them in the future. After all, he asks, "Who better to teach them 'bout this cruel world than I?," noting that he hopes they know that, whatever happened, "Daddy tried."

"Leanin' on You" goes further into gospel territory with its insistent sampled hook and lyrics that bear witness to each member's struggles and determination. This is the group at its most vulnerable, with almost all of their typical posturing dropped in favor of tender declarations of love and admissions of need. They embrace the gospel-soul continuum through the linked meanings of "leanin' on you" as a tribute to a steadfast partner and, in Bill's verse, a declaration of faith in God. Bill credits his faith with helping him pull through depression, drugs, and violence, as well as the challenges created by his size. He asks, "Why did God make my brother so tall and me a dwarf?" Sensing a shift into mawkishness, he assures listeners that this is "no 'poor little me' song," dismissing the pity and pathology with which earlier critics treated him. But, as on "I Tried," he insists that listeners confront the reality of how his height made him more of a target even as he needed to escape: "Everywhere you go, people point, people laugh, people stare." He quickly (and not entirely believably) says that because "they don't care," "I don't care," before noting that without his faith he'd surely be headed for hell for how he used to react to gawking and other insults.

Bushwick Bill's verse on "Leanin' on You" foreshadowed his next album, *My Testimony of Redemption* (2009), the last released during his lifetime. The album's gospel-rap seemed like a left turn. After two decades of hardcore rhymes, a sudden shift to Christian messages struck some as an odd and perhaps cynical shift. But Bill pointed out in numerous interviews that God had always been present in his recordings, whether as a source of strength or a symbol of struggle. And he also noted that spiritual work had been central to his life as Richard Shaw before Bushwick Bill ever existed. After all, he had come to Houston for a visit after graduating from Bible college and had planned to become a missionary, but the next thing he knew, he was wowing the crowds at the Rhinestone Wrangler.[5] Even after embracing a secular life, Bill remained committed to biblical teachings. "He really impressed me with the knowledge he had when the word of God was concerned," James Prince remembered. "He was almost like a Bible scholar, or a walking bible."[6] "His whole life's purpose," Yung KNXW said, was to do God's work, which extended into personal encounters with those he met on the road: "He gave them advice, he gave them light, and he gave them something to help with their life. He gave them ideas to help them further themselves, and that's what God's work is."[7]

Bill also used the Bible to offer another defense for his graphic rhymes. Just as he had invoked horror movies and opera, he now referenced biblical stories that he knew by chapter and verse. "If people think that I can't rap [now] like what they heard on Geto Boys," he said in 2013, "they haven't read Deuteronomy 28." Quoting a verse about a woman eating a child in secret, Bill noted a similarity between the phases of his career: "It's blessing and cursing." Negotiating the balance between "blessing" and "cursing" defines *My Testimony of Redemption* and the new phase that Bill hoped it would launch. As he reminded one interviewer, "God never said you'd be perfect."[8]

My Testimony of Redemption is a gospel remix of Bushwick Bill's entire career, a series of Sunday sermons based around a mix of Bible verses and his classic songs. "I traded Chuckwick into being a Jesus Freak," he raps on the title track, which follows the narrative beats of "Ever So Clear" as it traces his biography from Jamaica (complete with toasting) to being "a little underestimated kid, growing up in Brooklyn" to Geto Boys fame and ultimate misfortune. He references his shortness throughout the album, whether noting the teasing he faced as a child or, on the organ-drenched "Goin' to the River," how he tried to be "the drunkest, shortest cat in the club" to overcompensate.

Bill also used his famous songs to mark his departure from his old life. Over a heavy-metal beat, "No More Child's Play" references Corinthians and Bill's own horror-rap past. "Don't you remember? I be the one they used to call Chuckie, but representing Satan didn't do nothing for me," so now he's "a brand new preacher, the rap game teacher." He stays "brand new" on "Renewed Mind," which speeds up the track from "Mind Playing Tricks on Me" to offer a respectful goodbye to his Geto Boys days because there's "no more playing tricks on my renewed mind." Although he promises that he's not here to "separate the sinners from the Christians," he assures listeners that "if your mind's playing tricks on you, follow me."

Alongside his role as a "brand new preacher," Bill identified himself as a "rap game teacher" by offering commentary on hip-hop's past and present. The album begins with this message, starting with an "Intro" that reminds rappers that they are role models "whether they like it or not," and continuing into "Takin' It Back." This song, which bounces over an old-school beat, calls out rappers for pretending to be "pimpin'" when they actually have a loving wife and children "who you're trying to raise right." He says that the "record company" is the one who's really doing the exploitation, and he urges rappers to think of themselves as teachers in the manner of Chuck D, N.W.A. member Eazy E, and others he name-checks in the opening verse.

(He even throws in a Houston tribute, singing the chorus in a bass register reminiscent of the slowed-down productions of H-Town legend DJ Screw.)

Bill's criticism of modern-day rap excess is convenient given that he helped create gangsta and horrorcore and benefited from their growth in the marketplace. Even if it's sincere, the criticism of young rappers can't help but seem a bit like shaming given Bill's extremity in classic Geto Boys tracks and how eloquently he defended rap in the 1990s. Despite this, Bill's advice comes off less as "back in my day" hectoring and more like "back in the day" encouragement for the next cohort from someone who experienced both the triumphs and the pitfalls of rap stardom.

An even clearer example of this teaching occurred on the 2007 VH1 reality competition *Ego Trip's the (White) Rapper Show.* In one episode Bill served as guest mentor to a team of aspiring white hip-hop hopefuls. He was wearing a Hannibal Lecter mask as he was introduced, but his involvement bore little resemblance to the horrorcore antics that made him infamous. In a moment laden with symbolism, Bill takes off the nightmarish disguise before offering generous and thoughtful assistance to one of the groups competing in a team challenge. Together they record "Old School Music," a joyous ode to hip-hop's roots to which Bill contributes an autobiographical verse about how rap helped him find his way as a short kid in Brooklyn. He even shows off some breakdance moves in the video created for the song, which the team raps in front of a graffitied wall, and Bill sports an Afro wig and large sunglasses.[9] Despite his Houston identity, Bill's appearance on the show was to authenticate the contestants' connection to the New York roots of hip-hop culture. His team won the challenge.

Bill's mentorship of aspiring rappers extended across his albums, his guest appearances, and his work with other artists behind the scenes. Even the prevalence of posse cuts on his later solo albums could be interpreted as an effort to lift up lesser-known artists. It also extended into his everyday life. In 1994 he was sitting in the Houston airport when he was approached by a thirteen-year-old white kid named Paul Slayton, who later became hitmaking producer Paul Wall, and they chatted for several minutes. "I've thought about this over the years, and I truly believe this was the seed in me that would grow into [my career as Paul Wall]," he told Andrew Dansby after Bill's death. "I definitely was inspired by Bushwick in many ways. But most personal to me was how he treated people."[10]

The recording of *My Testimony of Redemption*, Bill's commitment to sobriety, and his increasingly stable family life seemed to signal a new chapter, but Bill soon faced further troubles. Following the death of Lonnie Mack, a close friend from Houston who had helped launch his career, Bill relapsed and was arrested in Atlanta for drug possession. During processing, authorities learned that Richard Shaw, who had immigrated to the United States with his parents in the mid-1970s, was not a US citizen. The recently launched Immigration and Customs Enforcement threatened to deport Bill, who had multiple criminal convictions, to either England or Canada.[11] Although he had arrived in the United States thanks to more open immigration policies, now he was being threatened because of new, punitive immigration laws.

Bill was not deported, but the arrest stalled whatever momentum *My Testimony of Redemption* had created. For the next several years, he maintained a relatively low profile, usually performing solo but occasionally on Geto Boys reunion tours. He also appeared on podcasts and gave interviews where he told stories and offered insights. He continued to battle addiction, admitting to one of his children that "I drink because I'm angry."[12] And he raised his family, including one son, Javon Boutte, who started rapping in 2014 as Yung KNXW.

The physical resemblance of father and son is striking. "At the end of the day I look just like my dad," KNXW noted, and though he is taller than Bill, some early coverage noted that he is shorter than average. Perhaps due to their physical similarity, he insisted that he "didn't want to just lean on that or depend on the fact that I'm Bushwick's son or call myself, Lil Bushwick."[13] As KXNW began exploring the possibility of his own rap career, his father encouraged both his creativity and his business savvy. "He told me, he said, 'look Javon, I made every mistake you can possibly make in this industry. Listen to me — make sure you sign with your ASCAP, get your royalties . . . make sure you copyright this and that.' Ever since then, since 17 years old,

I've been getting royalties in my ASCAP."[14] They collaborated early in KNXW's career, including Bushwick bringing him onstage at a triumphant performance he gave at the SXSW Festival in 2018. But both were careful to make sure that KNXW established his own creative lane rather than just exist in Bushwick Bill's long shadow. "There can't be another, Bushwick Bill," KNXW said in a 2018 interview. "I can look like him, rhyme like him and have his mannerisms, but at the end of the day, there is only one Bushwick Bill and there is only one, YK."[15]

In 2019, Yung KNXW released "Badu Vibe," a duet with Bill that emphasizes their love and collaboration. The cover photo features him as a toddler, hugging his father in front of a birthday cake, both with huge grins on their faces, and the song opens with Bill addressing both the audience and his son. "Listen to the young 'un, and he's gonna tell you how it is. Don't let them despise you because of your youth." At the end, Bushwick offers a loose verse that riffs on a poignant image: "The afterlife? What after life? Sure, after life," and with his voice drifting into falsetto, he ends with a haunting declaration, "I'm free," hanging onto the final syllable as it floats over the beat.

Bill recorded that verse in late 2018, but KNXW thinks his father knew what was coming. "He just prophesized a lotta stuff; the man was just super-intelligent."[16] In January 2019, Bill was diagnosed with stage 4 pancreatic cancer, a condition he made public in March. "It's not like I'm afraid of dying," he told *TMZ*, "because—if anybody knows anything about me from 'Ever So Clear,' you know, I died and came back already. . . . So I know what it's like on the other side. So that's not what it's really about. It's about life, and loving life, and being there for family." He also announced that he was recording three new albums to ensure that his children would be financially secure. "Old music will sell, yes, but if I have new music for them . . . at least they'll have residual income from those things. Instead of just knowing that I'm their dad and my old records are selling, that publishing belongs to someone else. I'd rather know for sure that I did my part."[17]

It's not clear how much he got done, but KNXW recalls him finishing "seventy-plus songs" before his time ran out.[18] Talking with radio personality Sway after his father's death, KNXW said that Bill used his last music to address the constant questions about how he felt during his final months and whether he would be able to keep his commitments—the kind of queries that frustrate people with chronic or debilitating illnesses. (KNWX recalls that Bill's response was "What you expect me to feel like? I'm in pain constantly, every single day.") In addition, KNXW said that his father's final music engages with "people's perspectives of him being Bushwick Bill, and them seeing him as not Richard Shaw whatsoever."[19]

The tracks that emerged from Bill's final sessions reflect these new considerations and continue the self-narrativization that he made central to his work. If his life and body were going to be the subject of misrepresentation or sensationalism (even within his own band), then he would rewrite his story around a more honest and multi-layered perspective that included the jokester persona that Scarface loved and the "midget rap" that Willie D had noticed, but also the survivor and social critic.[20] His final releases arrive at this conclusion with wisdom and resignation.

"Hard Times," which features Lil Flip, Chris Waters, and Tyna, is a call-and-response memoir based on "Times Is Hard" from *Phantom of the Rapra*. Surrounded by younger artists, Bill relates the pain and perseverance that marked his life's work. In the first verse he admits that he "had no filter on my physical, no cap off on my mental" as he tells his life story, by then a familiar text to anyone following Bill's work. But this time the story of how he went from short kid to worldwide star to broken man to survivor oozes with the awareness that these would be among his last words.

This is even more evident on "Clear So Ever," which flips the title of his defining solo anthem in order to assess his legacy. Over a slow-rolling beat, Bill describes how cancer had clarified his longer status as an outcast and misfit and his question about whether he "was really supposed to be on this planet Earth." But he also uses it to sharpen concerns about the fake friends he gained while famous. He contends with how to feel about "everybody callin' me who never called me before. They tellin' me they love me and all that, but really I'm just wishin' they would fall back." While this echoes his previous observations about fame, he works in a pointed criticism of the US health care system: "Nobody concernin' about my income, my outcome, while these doctors are takin' me for all I got and then some." He promises he will face cancer with God at his side. "No farewell for Bushwick," he assures listeners. "God got me."

Only a month after announcing his cancer diagnosis, Richard Shaw died at the age of fifty-two at a medical facility in Colorado. In the aftermath, hip-hop artists and fans offered their recollections, and he was the subject of extended profiles in mainstream news outlets for the first time. The tributes included memories from collaborators and influences, including Three 6 Mafia's Juicy J and fellow Texas rap titan Bun B, as well as fans who proclaimed Bill's importance to the culture and to themselves. Even Public Enemy's Chuck D, whose rhymes led to "Size Ain't Shit" and thus Bushwick Bill's career, paid homage. In comments to the *Houston Chronicle*, he called Bill "an icon and a standout character" and claimed that he "probably had one of the highest IQs of any rapper I've known."[21]

The most poignant tribute came in the 2020 music video for "Hard Times," which is structured around footage of his ashes being scattered by family and friends, including his parents and children, all dressed in Bushwick Bill memorial T-shirts. (Yung KNXW kept some of his father's ashes, which he wears in a vial around his neck.) Amid these scenes are shots of dancers and guest rappers in their

Bushwick Bill shirts performing in front of superimposed images of Bill working in the recording studio. By intermingling tributes to the art and the man who created it, "Hard Times" insists that we remember both in a way that doesn't reduce them to narratives that are about only difference or sickness, or outrage and excess, but that honor all aspects of his art and identity. In the video's last shot, an artist puts finishing touches on a Bushwick Bill memorial mural, a fitting tribute for a hip-hop legend who began as a graffiti artist himself. Next to a beautifully rendered portrait, the artist has painted three words that the camera lingers on before fading to black.

"LITTLE BIG MAN."

GREATEST SHOWMEN

In December 2017, P. T. Barnum made an unexpected return to the center of US popular culture with the release of the film *The Greatest Showman*. The musical stars Hugh Jackman in the title role as a bootstraps-pulling version of Barnum whose love of theater and spirit of perseverance helped him create a career in show business in spite of numerous obstacles. Along with him come the freaks, here presented as initially unwilling to be exploited by Barnum but eventually convincing him to keep going and follow his dreams. He believes in *them*, so they believe in *him*. The spirit of self-empowerment that suffuses the film extends to the soundtrack, which effectively mixes old-fashioned show tune gusto and modern pop flourishes. The centerpiece is "This Is Me," sung first by Keala Settle, who portrays the Bearded Lady, and later taken up by all the performers and Barnum himself. It's a spirited anthem of self-acceptance that seems assured of a long life in karaoke bars, drag shows, and school concerts.

One of the film's central figures, and the freak who earns the most prominent narrative attention, is General Tom

Thumb, portrayed by Sam Humphrey. The film does an admirable job of re-creating Charles Stratton's initial skepticism of Barnum and gives him some agency in deciding to join the troupe and adopt the character. But all complexity is washed away when Barnum's redemption becomes the narrative arc. In one scene late in the film, a distraught Barnum is drowning his sorrows in a tavern when a familiar pair of small feet walk along the bar. It's Charles Stratton, who stands at eye level with the seated Barnum and gives him words of encouragement before everyone launches into a production number. It's all very inspiring. And like much of the film, it's all so much bullshit.[1]

Watching *The Greatest Showman* in a crowded theater, I grew exasperated not only with the film's historical inaccuracies (which were documented extensively by justifiably annoyed critics) but also by the audience's predictable reactions.[2] The adventures of Barnum and his gang were greeted with laughter, cheers, and (worst of all) *aww*s. My observations at the screening were reconfirmed as the film and soundtrack became a phenomenon and "This Is Me" even heart-warmed its way to the Oscar stage.

The film wasn't even close to the worst presentation of short-statured people that I've seen on screen, nor was it close to the worst example of abled-pleasing "inspiration porn" I've witnessed. As developed by writer and activist Stella Young, the phrase *inspiration porn* describes the pairing of a disabled person "doing something completely ordinary" with empowering messages such as "Your excuse is invalid" or "The only disability is a bad attitude." As Young notes, these images exist "so that non-disabled people can put their worries into perspective" by assuming that "the people in them have terrible lives, and that it takes some extra kind of pluck or courage to live them."[3] Young's formulation resonates deeply with people like me who recognize such interactions from our own lives and the cultural representations of disabled people. *The Greatest Showman* exploits this impulse, though I appreciated the way that the early scenes with Charles Stratton acknowledged the exploitation inherent in Barnum's spectacle and how Humphrey imbued the role with quiet dignity.

But, particularly as any ambivalence got glossed over in favor of crowd-pleasing earworms and feel-good nonsense, it was supremely frustrating to see these well-worn tropes played out with fresh razzle-dazzle. It was infuriating to see Barnum's justifiably tarnished reputation be rehabilitated by a magnetic star and a rose-colored narrative. And it was disappointing to realize that on top of everything else that disabled folks have to wade through, *The Greatest Showman* added another layer of adorable bullshit to how our experiences are expressed in pop culture. And it featured a short guy as a primary symbol of disabled pluck and perseverance. I knew that the next time somebody called me an inspiration, they may well have "This Is Me" humming in the back of their mind.

Sam Humphrey's performance in *The Greatest Showman* came at a moment when representations of people with dwarfism had never been more prominent — or more fraught. TLC's hit show *Little People, Big World* and its spinoffs present an extended attempt to consider the lives of little people both within and against an inaccessible world. But its popularity, which rests on regular-sized people's fascination with the everyday lives of people with dwarfism, led many to condemn it as another harmful manifestation of post-freak show gawk.[4] Also drawing public attention to dwarfism were Verne Troyer's performances as Mini-Me in the *Austin Powers* franchise, which reinforced childlike stereotypes even as Troyer's reputation for hard partying counteracted that impression. He died by suicide in 2018.[5] Similarly, comical figures such as *Jackass*'s Wee Man and WWE's Hornswoggle use their size to emphasize the spectacle (and hilarity) of their physical stunts even as they adopted a badass look and attitude both on- and off-screen. Peter Dinklage has become perhaps the most prominent and celebrated short actor in the history of film and television; not only has he had major roles in *Game of Thrones*, *The Station Agent*, and *Elf*, but all of these performances (and others) feature Dinklage engaging with the reality of his height while not falling into tragic or inspirational narratives. He has also used his fame to speak out against hatred. After winning a Golden Globe in 2012, he told the audience to look up Martin Henderson, a victim of dwarf-tossing, and he has amplified the voices of those who seek to dismantle the dehumanization of short-statured people.[6]

All of this imbued my reactions to *The Greatest Showman*. I wanted a more accurate narrative. But more than that, I wanted a better fiction. I wanted a story that downplayed the rah-rah in favor of the complex and affecting stories that could be told through a fuller examination of Barnum's performers, especially, though not only, the short man who started it all. I also wanted more simple pleasures. In one specific fantasy I imagined that while standing atop that bar and facing a forlorn Barnum, General Tom Thumb would have taken the opportunity to kick that motherfucker in the face.

What I wanted was Bushwick Bill. I wanted a disabled intervention that would be both piercing and profane, mixing hard reality with hilarious exaggeration. I wanted the fierceness of Bill's politics mixed with his refusal to tone it down. I wanted the hard-fought self-acceptance that Kiana Fitzgerald identified in his work, rather than the cheap version proffered by *Greatest Showman*. I wanted Bill's sexuality, his anger, his humor, his outrageousness, his tenderness, his messiness, his lack of respectability, and all the rest. I wanted his defiance of the pity that Robert Bogdan notes often characterizes the "presentation mode for people with physical, mental, and behavioral differences."[7] I wanted the multiple voicings of disabled experience that Bill presented in his work as way to counteract abled desires. And I wanted his brilliant talent.

I didn't find Bushwick Bill in *The Greatest Showman*, and I was probably silly for hoping that I would. But I do find him elsewhere. I hear him in the work of Yung KXNW, both in his terrific music and in his keeping of his father's legacy. In 2019, after Bill died, KNXW released "Times Still Hard," a riff on the song that Bill introduced on *Phantom of the Rapra* and brought back for his final single. The cover of KNXW's new single juxtaposes photos of KNXW and Bushwick Bill from his performing prime, but even though Bill is listed as a featured artist, he doesn't appear on the track itself. Still, between the cover, title, and subject matter, Bushwick Bill haunts the track. The two men look great together.

I wish I could hear Bushwick Bill's influence in a new generation of short-statured people rocking the mic in mainstream pop music, but this is not the case. The only prominent small performers who have emerged in recent years have been sideshow adjuncts to white rap-adjacent artists. Kid Rock's sidekick, Joe C, and Two-Foot Fred from country-rap gonzos Big & Rich are both dancing hype men in the model of Little Billy rather than rappers with the furious rhymes of Bushwick Bill. (Two-Foot Fred is actually part of a carnival that is used by Big & Rich as their performance motif.) But I absolutely hear Bushwick Bill through the continuing significance of the Geto Boys' music, as well as contemporary rap's willingness to engage issues of mental health and a broader move toward body positivity that has included increased (though still contested) space for non-normative and conventionally "unattractive" people as both subjects and objects of sexual desire.

Although their presence in the mainstream remains limited, disabled rappers, just like other disabled people, are everywhere, offering their compelling, defiant, moving, and sometimes hilarious remixes of hip-hop's language and sonic markers. One of my favorites is Wheelchair Sports Camp, led by Denver-based emcee Kalyn Heffernan, who has the same bone condition that I do. In 2016 she released an album called *No Big Deal*, a winking reminder of Bushwick Bill's *Little Big Man*. The album is filled with pointed examinations of disabled life delivered with a fluid, skittering delivery over bubbling beats. "I got over being so pissed with my own anatomy," she raps at one point. "Now casually living life in all its majesty." Several songs riff directly on rap tropes. In "Talk My Way Out" she notes that "my wheelchair weighs a ton," a reference to Public Enemy's early track "My Uzi Weighs a Ton." "Scooter Pack" is a tribute to fellow short rapper Mac Tay Capone, whose gangsta reputation made him a threat on the streets ("What he lacked in height he made up in arrogance") and a star once his videos rolled out on social media.

On the closing track of *No Big Deal*, "Hard Out Here for a Gimp," Heffernan goes even further in flipping the script. Here she uses the Three 6 Mafia–referencing hook (based on their Oscar-winning theme song to the film *Hustle and Flow*) to riff on societal inaccessibility ("There's a stairway to heaven, so how the hell we gonna get in?"), personal marginalization (she references 2Pac's "All Eyez on Me" to signal her hypervisibility), and an insistence on a defiant, celebratory, and sexual identity. At one point she even calls herself the "inspiration-porn star."[8] I hear Bushwick Bill in Wheelchair Sports Camp, Mac Tay Capone, and all the disabled artists in the worldwide underground. I wish they had the audience that he did.

Most of these artists are associated with the subgenre krip-hop, a term coined by activist and artist Leroy F. Moore, Jr., in 2007.[9] "When I was growing up," Moore remembered, "my father had a huge record collection of blues and soul, and in the 1970s I listened to all of it. I noticed there were a lot of disabled Black male singers and wanted to learn more about them. In my research I found that the industry has always had trouble supporting and promoting musicians with disabilities, especially Black musicians."[10] Moore's love of rap and his awareness of the limited opportunities for disabled artists led to the development of Krip-Hop Nation, a collective that gives disabled artists a powerful space of organization and amplification. "Krip-Hop Nation doesn't want you to feel good/inspire but wants you to feel uncomfortable/angry!" Moore declared, and the group promotes this mission through publications, performances, broadcasts, and a long-running series of mixtapes.[11]

Krip-Hop Nation is one of the most powerful articulations of the connection between hip-hop politics and disability justice. Prior to founding the organization, Moore was already a longtime activist working to increase the awareness of racial justice within disability advocacy, and Krip-Hop Nation reflects this mission in a rap-specific context. The group's platform includes everything from a condemnation of bigoted language to the recognition of "disabled ancestors," as well as a disability-centered version of hip-hop politics. "A longstanding and pivotal theme," Mikko Koivisto notes, "is the mistreatment of people with disabilities by law enforcement officers and the legal system."[12] Krip-Hop Nation has released brutality-specific mixtapes, and many of their affiliated artists (including Wheelchair Sports Camp and Mac Tay Capone) have insisted on links between these movements on both ideological and strategic levels.[13] As Rebecca Adelman has discussed, the affinity between hip-hop and disability justice is not hard to understand because both "address a set of bodies that have been repeatedly categorized as deficient or immoderate by various discourses and cultural norms."[14] The work of Krip-Hop Nation embodies and soundtracks the intersections between disability and other aspects of hip-hop's political challenge.

Koivisto has also suggested that Krip-Hop Nation might seem oppositional to Bushwick Bill. "Bill — and the genre he represents, horrorcore — might be considered a target of the critique posed by Krip Hop Nation on the mainstream hip hop industry, insofar as he uses openly misogynist rhetoric and pairs violent behaviour with mental disability." But he also notes that Bill's "excessive and overdriven exploitation of the most extreme stereotypes of blackness, disability and violence might function, on another level, as a resistance to . . . the very stereotypes it employs," especially when paired with the more reflective vision of "Ever So Clear" and his gospel work.[15] Leroy Moore, Jr., himself has honored Bushwick Bill as a Krip-Hop forefather.[16]

Koivisto is one of several writers who have invoked Bushwick Bill in recent scholarship on disability, race, and culture. These writers not only build on the example of Krip-Hop Nation but also on the legacies of Christopher Bell, a foundational scholar who argued that disability studies, like disability activism, could not be legitimate without the presence of Black people and critical race theory. "The work of reading black and disabled bodies is not only recovery work," Bell wrote, "but work that requires a willingness to deconstruct the systems that would keep those bodies in separate spheres."[17] Bell's call has produced a growing response among a new cohort of scholars, many of whom — including Koivisto, Moya Bailey, and Anna Hinton — have contended with Bushwick Bill and other unruly rap figures as part of a larger critique of both hip-hop and disability studies. They argue that hip-hop demonstrates the limitations of what Bailey calls "the ineffective dichotomy of positive and negative representation" by using "the liminal spaces of hip-hop" to enact a "reappropriation of ableist language . . . that departs from generally accepted disparaging connotations."[18]

The reappropriative impulse more broadly motivates the new generation of disabled writers, artists, and activists who build on earlier radicalism and remix it through brash millennial/Gen-Z brilliance.[19] Beyond reclaiming words such as *crip* and rejecting respectability politics, this cohort has transformed understandings of disability using a wide range of strategies, from street-level activism to social media. On Twitter, for example, disabled folks organize and converse around electoral campaigns such as #CripTheVote (created by Gregg Baratan, Andrew Pulrang, and Alice Wong), cultural interventions such as #DisabilitySoWhite (the work of Vilissa Thompson), and crowdsourced testimonies such as #AbledsAreWeird (produced by Imani Barbarin).[20] These and other content creators build accessible spaces where disabled people can have affirming conversations that exist outside of abled gatekeepers and extend into other spaces of art and politics. There are far too many names to mention, and new voices emerge every day. At their best, Twitter and other digital spaces reflect the fierce and funny liberation that defines the ongoing fight for justice. I find Bushwick Bill here too.

Of course, Twitter is also a primary vehicle for the most prominent current user of ableist slurs. Donald Trump's endless cascade of insults includes numerous derogatory nicknames, and the ones he gave Marco Rubio, Mike

Bloomberg, and others include "Lil" or "Mini," obvious jabs at their masculinity. Trump's gleeful use of these diminutives is, for short folks, a painful reminder of taunting bullies and the way that many people (not just Trump) think about us. I imagine that Bushwick Bill, who burned a picture of Bob Dole and told George Bush to go screw himself, would offer a particularly scathing takedown of Trump's demeaning comments and hateful politics.

I find Bushwick Bill reverberating in the chorus of voices—of activists, artists, scholars, teachers, and people in all walks of life—who refuse to tolerate the demeaning stereotypes that short people and other disabled folks have learned to survive. Rosemarie Garland-Thomson reminds us that "disabled people must use charm, intimidation, ardor, deference, humor or entertainment to relieve nondisabled people of their discomfort. Those of us with disabilities are supplicants and minstrels, striving to create valued representations of ourselves in our relations with the nondisabled majority."[21] Too often, this is our experience. It's my experience.

So I try to find Bushwick Bill in my own life. He has proved a crucial, surprising role model for me as I've thought about my own difference and the way it shapes my experiences. In Bill's songs I hear the defiance of the disabled activists who paved the way for my generation and those who are now taking up the cause for the future. I hear the critique of American society that includes disability justice, even as many social movements still do not con-

sider it or only pay it lip service. I hear the humor that becomes both weapon and coping mechanism, and the sexual
desire that is too often ignored or fetishized. And I hear the
recognition that even with all the ammunition we possess,
there are still moments when it all feels like too much.

Garland-Thomson's use of *minstrel* is worth revisiting.
It is impossible to understand Bushwick Bill outside of his
particular experiences, not only as a disabled person but as
a disabled Black man. I'm aware that as a white man, despite my best efforts, there is surely some exoticism that
goes into my love of this Black artist. When I bob my head
to "Mind Playing Tricks on Me," quote my favorite lines
from "Size Ain't Shit," reflexively excuse the misogyny and
homophobia present in too many of his songs, or more generally proclaim Bushwick Bill as a role model, I risk giving
in to the minstrel or freak-show temptation of projecting
my own white fears and fantasies onto a Black body, even
if it shares an important marker with mine.

I also try to remember a connected reality. Would I feel
as close to a short-statured rapper or other musician who is
female or nonbinary? And given the severe limitations of
the record industry and cultural marketplace, would I even
get a chance? The narrow space for disabled performers is
even narrower for those who are not cisgender men, and
I recognize my affinity for Bushwick Bill as a product of
masculine identification and a consequence of structural
gender disparity. So it's fucked up and complex: my own
disability doesn't render me immune from racist or sexist

thoughts even, or perhaps especially, when they're dressed up in the tempting fetish of positive stereotypes. In this sense, Bushwick Bill matters deeply to me, and to the rest of the world, because he forces me to confront those very associations. In the work he created, whether prophetic or problematic, he demanded a recognition of disabled lives that extends far beyond the acceptable bounds of ableist or racist preconceptions, including those I may have absorbed.

With that said, I still find Bushwick Bill's defiance of the cultural narratives surrounding short-statured folks to be deeply liberating and resonant with my own experiences. I've experienced hateful comments and discrimination, of course. I've been stared at, laughed at, left out, called names, assumed to be helpless, and asked astonishingly personal questions about my sex life (which is usually rooted in the assumption that I either don't have one or have one that is really fascinating). But you know what's somehow worse than all that? The well-meaning motherfuckers. The people who think it's adorable to watch me do things. The folks who come out of nowhere and want to hear my story or have me tell it, who trot me out as a good example, who offer congratulations I don't deserve and praise I haven't earned because I've somehow inspired them by my example — and whose inquiring minds do not signal hostility, but a surprise and wonder that are no less demeaning.

In all his messy complexity, and mine, Bushwick Bill has

taught me something about how to communicate a proper response. He taught me that it's okay to rage, mourn, and question my physicality even as I embrace it. He taught me that the refusal of our "extraordinary bodies" to abide by physical or social expectations is a *good* thing because it gives us an expertise that so-called normals don't share and helps us figure out their true intentions. He taught me how to insist on equal treatment and how to resist the *aww*. He taught me that if you can't dance like nobody's watching, then you might as well dance like *everyone* is. He taught me to put on the armor, crank up the bass, and remind everyone—most of all myself—that size ain't shit, and fuck 'em if they say otherwise. And he taught me that sometimes it's necessary to look those clowns straight in the soul and laugh.

I honor Bushwick Bill for his significant contributions to hip-hop and popular music. I celebrate him for a life that defiantly affirmed the genius of disabled people. I praise him for his powerful resistance to an ableist and racist society. And I thank him for helping me make my way in an inaccessible world.

"When I became a rapper," he once said, "if you heard the name Bushwick Bill and heard my voice I promise you'd never forget that you'd heard me."[22]

I never will. And I hope you won't either.

ACKNOWLEDGMENTS

My parents, Ron and the late Lee Ann Hughes, convinced me from the beginning that size ain't shit. But they also helped me understand and embrace the disability that defined but did not encompass my identity or experiences. Along with my extended family, they created an accessible world the best they could, one that armed me with the courage, joy, humor, and compassion that I need. For that they have my deepest love and appreciation.

This book exists thanks to the inestimable work of Casey Kittrell, whose early encouragement and editorial guidance convinced me that there was a story to tell and that I could tell it. I'm also deeply appreciative to the series co-editors, Oliver Wang and Evelyn McDonnell, for their help, as well as Regina Bradley and Jack Hamilton, whose suggestions proved invaluable as the manuscript came together. And thanks to the whole University of Texas Press team.

Many folks helped make this book happen, some years before it existed. There are, of course, too many to mention, but I want to thank Rudy Aguilar, Charlie Alden, Danny Alexander, Simon Balto, Susannah Bartlow, John Bass, John Beifuss, Chanelle Benz, Brian Bischel, Kijan Bloomfield, Chris Brunt, Stephanie Cage, John Capista, Liz Carlson, Matt Cepress, Mike Cepress, Jeff Chang, Dan

Charnas, Justin Davis, Sarah Ifft Decker, Jerome Dotson, Steacy Easton, Stephanie Elsky, Nan Enstad, Tom Erlewine, K. T. Ewing, Piko Ewoodzie, John Floyd, Tanisha Ford, Daniel Frederick, Trudy Fredericks, Ari Friedlander, Tyler Fritts, Ernest Gibson, Robert Gordon, Eddie Hankins, Marjorie Hass, Jamey Hatley, Laura and Patrick Helper, Mike Heyliger, Jewly Hight, Jessica Hopper, Kendra Hotz, Jeff Jackson, Chris Jarvis, Hasan Jeffries, the late Doria Johnson, Loren Kajikawa, Tait Keller, Jeff and Jen Kollath, Kiese Laymon, Duane Loynes, Bill and Bobbie Malone, Dave Marsh, Amanda Martinez, Erica and Kevin McCool, Danielle McGuire, Charles McKinney, Iris Mercado, Bob Mehr, Leah Mirakhor, Chris Molanphy, Ryan Murphy, Raka Nandi, Samson Ndanyi, Jeff Ogbar, Evie Perry, Ann Powers, Tauheed Rahim II, Caryn Rose, Robert Saxe, Eric Schumacher-Rasmussen, Jo and Wyl Schuth, Dan Sharber, Alexander Shashko, Mark Simpson-Vos, RJ Smith, Alfred Soto, Heather Stur, Laura Taylor, Elizabeth Thomas, Joey Thompson, Karen Tongson, Tim Tyson, Greg and Lee Ann Venne, Elijah Wald, Eric Weisbard, Eric Wenninger, Craig Werner, Carl Wilson, Cookie Woolner, and Annie Zaleski. I am especially grateful to David Cantwell, Dave Gilbert, Zandria Robinson, and Tyina Steptoe, great friends and colleagues who each made a particularly significant contribution to my understanding of Bushwick Bill and my relationship to him. Thanks also to Caitlin Wood for last-minute help and long-term badassery, and to Angela Frederick and Ellen Samuels, two brilliant scholars whose work I have not cited here but whose ideas and friendship were both critical to how I understand disability and what it means to live as a disabled person.

Ari Eisenberg, another person who has greatly influenced my thinking about disability, has shaped my life in more ways than I can imagine. We bonded early over the Geto Boys, and Ari was the first person to ask what Bushwick Bill meant to me. I hope this book honors some of the piercing insight and soul-deep generosity that Ari brings to everything they do. I am so deeply lucky to witness their brilliance, humor, kindness, and radical commitment to justice. No matter what, we will always be family. This book is for them.

NOTES

A Note on Terminology

1. There are multiple medical causes of dwarfism, but the most common is achondroplasia.

2. The writer and activist Eugene Grant prefers the term *dwarf person* and has discussed his choice and the larger question of naming in several places. See his 2018 Twitter thread documented in Isobel Hamilton, "Writer and Activist Shares Twitter Thread about the Language People with Dwarfism Have to Deal With," *Mashable*, Mar. 1, 2018, https://mashable.com/2018/03/01/eugene-grant-thread-people-dwarfism-language/; see also Eugene Grant, "The Fearless Benjamin Lay: Activist, Abolitionist, Dwarf Person," in *Disability Visibility: First-Person Stories from the Twenty-First Century*, ed. Alice Wong (New York: Vintage, 2020), 229–231.

3. For more information on this question, see statements by Little People of America and Understanding Dwarfism, two of the preeminent advocacy organizations. Little People of America, "LPA Issues Statement to Abolish the 'M' Word," LPA online, Sept. 2015, https://www.lpaonline.org/the-m-word; Understanding Dwarfism, "What Is the Correct Terminology?," http://www.udprogram.com/correct-terminology.

Introduction

1. Tarbox Kiersted, "Bushwick Bill Rapped That He Had 'the Mind of a Lunatic.' Underneath, He Was Laughing," *Houston Chronicle*, June 14, 2019, https://www.houstonchronicle.com/local/gray-matters/article/Bushwick-Bill-rapped-that-he-had-the-mind-of-a-13998212.php.

2. Andrew Dansby, "Geto Boys' Bushwick Bill Dies," *Houston Chronicle*, June 10, 2019, https://www.houstonchronicle.com/entertainment/music/article/Geto-Boys-Bushwick-Bill-dies-13964959.php.

3. Rosemarie Garland-Thomson, *Staring: How We Look* (New York: Oxford University Press, 2009), 173.

4. Garland-Thomson, 172.

5. Garland-Thomson, *Extraordinary Bodies: Figuring Physical Disability in American Culture and Literature* (New York: Columbia University Press, 1997), 37.

6. George McKay, *Shakin' All Over: Popular Music and Disability* (Ann Arbor: University of Michigan Press, 2013), 2.

7. Joseph N. Straus, *Extraordinary Measures: Disability in Music* (New York: Oxford University Press, 2011).

8. See Eric Lott, *Love and Theft: Blackface Minstrelsy and the American Working Class* (New York: Oxford University Press, 1995).

9. Wilkins here notes Bill's similarity to Richard Pryor. See Dansby, "Geto Boys' Bushwick Bill Dies."

10. Rolf Potts, *The Geto Boys* (New York: Continuum, 2016), 28.

11. Garland-Thomson, *Extraordinary Bodies*, 11.

12. Shawna Kenney, "Geto Boy: An Interview with Bushwick Bill," *Pitchfork*, Sept. 8, 2015, https://pitchfork.com/thepitch/893-geto-boy-an-interview-with-bushwick-bill/.

13. Shea Serrano, "The H-Town Countdown, No. 16: Bushwick Bill's *Little Big Man*," *Houston Press*, Oct. 8, 2009, https://www.houstonpress.com/music/the-h-town-countdown-no-16-bushwick-bills-little-big-man-6529491.

How Little Billy Became Bushwick Bill

1. Lance Scott Walker, *Houston Rap Tapes: An Oral History of Bayou City Hip-Hop* (Austin: University of Texas Press, 2018), 47–48.

2. Brad Jordan and Benjamin Meadows Ingram, *Diary of a Madman: The Geto Boys, Life, Death, and the Roots of Southern Rap* (New York: Dey Street Books, 2015), 32.

3. James Prince, with Jasmine D. Waters, *The Art and Science of Respect: A Memoir by James Prince* (Houston: N-The-Water, 2018), 107.

4. "Murder Master Music Show," episode 618, *Blog Talk Radio*, June 26, 2019, https://www.blogtalkradio.com/murdermastermusicshow/2019/07/26/episode-618-yung-knxw/.

5. For more information on this period, see Jeff Chang, *Can't Stop Won't Stop: A History of the Hip-Hop Generation* (New York: Picador, 2005); and

Joseph C. Ewoodzie Jr., *Break Beats in the Bronx: Rediscovering Hip-Hop's Early Years* (Chapel Hill: University of North Carolina Press, 2015).

6. Maco Faniel, *Hip-Hop in Houston: The Origin and the Legacy* (Charleston, SC: History Press, 2013), 110.

7. "A few teachers call Bushwick a captivating personality who easily drew friends and girlfriends," Catherine Chriss wrote in the *Houston Chronicle* in 1992. "Others remember another side to him." See Chriss, "For Houston's Geto Boys, Anything Goes in the World of Gangsta Rap," *Houston Chronicle*, Apr. 5, 1992.

8. In an obituary, Jon Caramanica suggests that Bill "immersed himself" in these years. See Caramanica, "Bushwick Bill, Rapper Who Told Harrowing Tales in Geto Boys, Is Dead at 52," *New York Times*, June 10, 2019, https://www.nytimes.com/2019/06/10/obituaries/bushwick-bill -dead.html. In *Hip-Hop in Houston*, Maco Faniel identifies Bill as a member of the Linden Crash Crew dancers, and in a 2005 interview with *XXL Magazine* Bill recalled coming in second place in a 1982 competition behind a female dancer named Ladyflex. See Peter Relic, "The Return," *XXL Magazine* (January/February 2005), reprinted in *Da Capo Best Music Writing 2006*, ed. Mary Gaitskill and Daphne Carr, 231–239.

9. According to an interview in 1995, he even competed in a televised contest sponsored by the Swatch corporation. See The W and Mason Storm, interview with Bushwick Bill, July 10, 1995, http://www.the41online.com /bill.html. The artist Blake "KEO" Latham recalled Bill's graffiti name in an Instagram post that was subsequently mentioned by Shawn Setaro in his obituary. Setaro, "Bushwick Bill Can't Be Stopped," *Complex*, June 10, 2019, https://www.complex.com/music/2019/06/bushwick-bill-obituary.

10. "Murder Master Music Show," episode 618.

11. Bill even remembered being affiliated with Afrika Bambaataa's Zulu Nation, perhaps the most influential hip-hop organization to blend community support with creative expression. See The W and Mason Storm, interview with Bushwick Bill.

12. "Rap-a-Lot Founder J. Prince Remembers Bushwick Bill: 'He Was Almost Like a Bible Scholar,'" *Billboard*, June 10, 2019, https://www.billboard .com/articles/columns/hip-hop/8515201/bushwick-bill-j-prince -interview.

13. Walker, *Houston Rap Tapes*, 48.

14. Andy Langer, "Bushwick Bill: 'I'm Not Going to Allow People to Love Me for Who I'm Not,'" *Texas Monthly* podcast, June 10, 2019, https://www.texasmonthly.com/podcast/bushwick-bill-houston-hip-hop-geto-boys/.

15. Walker, *Houston Rap Tapes*, 43.

16. Tyina L. Steptoe, *Houston Bound: Culture and Color in a Jim Crow City* (Berkeley: University of California Press, 2016).

17. Steptoe, 4–5.

18. Jordan and Ingram, *Diary of a Madman*, 88.

19. Faniel, *Hip Hop in Houston*, 25.

20. Steptoe, *Houston Bound*, 68.

21. Prince, *Art and Science of Respect*, 19.

22. Jordan and Ingram, *Diary of a Madman*, 88.

23. Prince, *Art and Science of Respect*, 108.

24. Walker, *Houston Rap Tapes*, 40.

25. Bushwick's son says Bill also created choreography for the group. See "Murder Master Music Show," episode 618.

26. Langer, "Bushwick Bill."

27. Walker, *Houston Rap Tapes*, 40–41.

28. Walker, 41.

29. The East Coast did produce important artists in the early gangsta movement, including Boogie Down Productions, Kool G Rap, and Schoolly D, a Philadelphia-based artist often credited with recording the first gangsta track.

30. Eric Harvey has compellingly argued that the term *reality rap* reflects less an authentic view of real conditions and more the same mix of "hard-'hood realities with creative, cocksure fictions" that were elsewhere visible in the rise of early reality TV shows such as *COPS* and *America's Most Wanted*, both of which offered a similar mix of hyperrealistic documentation with exaggerated narratives of crime and punishment. See Eric Harvey, "Who Got The Camera? N.W.A.'s Embrace of 'Reality,' 1988–1992," *Pitchfork*, Mar. 31, 2015, https://pitchfork.com/thepitch/720-who-got-the-camera-nwas-embrace-of-reality-1988-1992/.

31. Perhaps unsurprisingly, this became a common pun for Bill throughout his career.

32. Prince, *Art and Science of Respect*, 110.

33. Walker, *Houston Rap Tapes*, 41.

34. Walker, 44.

35. Brian Coleman, *Check the Technique: Liner Notes for Hip-Hop Junkies* (New York: Random House, 2009), 224.

36. Jordan and Ingram, *Diary of a Madman*, 43.

37. Faniel, *Hip-Hop in Houston*, 114.

38. Jordan and Ingram, *Diary of a Madman*, 41.

39. Roni Sarig, *Third Coast: OutKast, Timbaland, and How Hip-Hop Became a Southern Thing* (New York: Da Capo, 2007), 43.

40. Sarig, 47.

41. Willie D, quoted in John Nova Lomax, "The Geto Boys and Public Enemy, 25 Years Ago," *Houstonia*, Aug. 28, 2013, https://www.houstoniamag.com /arts-and-culture/2013/08/the-geto-boys-and-public-enemy-together -august-2013.

42. Sarig, *Third Coast*, 47; Faniel, *Hip-Hop in Houston*, 122.

43. Raheem was one of the original Ghetto Boys, rapping on "Car Freak." See Walker, *Houston Rap Tapes*, 79.

Bum-Rush the Freak Show

1. Straus, *Extraordinary Measures*.

2. Betty Adelson, *The Lives of Dwarfs: Their Journey from Public Curiosity toward Social Liberation* (New Brunswick, NJ: Rutgers University Press, 2005), 3–20.

3. Adelson, 21–22.

4. Garland-Thomson, *Extraordinary Bodies*, 64–65.

5. Garland-Thomson, 65.

6. Garland-Thomson, 65.

7. See, for example, Benjamin Reiss, "P. T. Barnum, Joice Heth, and Antebellum Spectacles of Race," *American Quarterly* 51, no. 1 (March 1999): 84–85.

8. Adelson notes that one European traveler wrote that "the Yoruba viewed dwarfs as 'uncanny in some rather undefined way, having a form similar to certain potent spirits who carry out the will of the gods.'" See Adelson, *Lives of Dwarfs*, 8–9; see also Walter Johnson, *Soul By Soul: Life Inside the Antebellum Slave Market* (Cambridge, MA: Harvard University Press, 1999).

9. Dea H. Boster, *African American Slavery and Disability: Bodies, Property, and Power in the Antebellum South, 1800–1860* (New York: Routledge, 2012), 3.

10. David Gerber, "The 'Careers' of People Exhibited in Freak Shows: The Problem of Volition and Valorization," in *Freakery: Cultural Spectacles of the Extraordinary Body*, ed. Rosemarie Garland-Thomson (New York: New York University Press, 1996), 49.

11. Adelson, *Lives of Dwarfs*, 27.

12. Garland-Thomson, *Extraordinary Bodies*, 59. See also Reiss, "P. T. Barnum," as well as Reiss's book *The Showman and the Slave: Race, Death, and Memory in Barnum's America* (Cambridge, MA: Harvard University Press, 2010).

13. Garland-Thomson, *Extraordinary Bodies*, 69; Leonard Cassuto, "Freak," in *Keywords in Disability Studies*, ed. Rachel Adams et al. (New York: New York University Press, 2015), 86–87.

14. Reiss, "P. T. Barnum," 87.

15. Straus (*Extraordinary Measures*) notes that these categories have been linked to the rise of the "medical model" of disability and the accompanying decline in the belief that disability represents divine judgment or personal failure.

16. Terry Rowden, *The Songs of Blind Folk: African American Musicians and the Cultures of Blindness* (Ann Arbor: University of Michigan Press, 2009), 15.

17. Rowden, 21.

18. Straus, *Extraordinary Measures*.

19. Rowden chronicles this history throughout *Souls of Blind Folk*.

20. Laurie Stras has published several important works on the Boswell sisters. The most important for this book are "'Who Told You That Lie?': Picturing Connie Boswell," in *Re-framing Representations of Women: Figuring, Fashioning, Portraiting, and Telling in the "Picturing" Women Project*, ed. Susan Shifrin (London: Ashgate, 2008); and Stras, "Sing a Song of Difference: Connie Boswell and a Discourse of Disability in Jazz," *Popular Music* 28, no. 3 (October 2009).

21. McKay, *Shakin' All Over*, 38.

22. McKay, 42.

23. Dury's first band, Kilburn and the High Roads, consciously featured a variety of non-normative bodies, including a drummer with

nonfunctioning legs and a bassist whom Dury referred to as a "midget" (see McKay, 45).

24. McKay, 38.

25. McKay, 49–51.

26. McKay, 42.

27. "Dirty-old-man-in-a-mac" quoted in McKay, 42; Straus, *Extraordinary Measures*.

28. McKay, *Shakin' All Over*, 38.

"Size Ain't Shit"

1. Potts, *Geto Boys*, 45–46.

2. Gerber, "'Careers,'" 49.

3. David Fricke, "Randy Newman: My Life in 15 Songs," *Rolling Stone*, https://www.rollingstone.com/music/music-lists/randy-newman-my-life-in-15-songs-202825/short-people-204315/.

4. Joanna Powell, "Randy Newman's 'Short People,'" *Entertainment Weekly*, Dec. 11, 1992, https://ew.com/article/1992/12/11/randy-newmans-short-people/.

5. Adelson, *Lives of Dwarfs*, 319.

6. Gerber, "'Careers,'" 50.

7. Adelson, *Lives of Dwarfs*, 319.

8. See Nell Irvin Painter's discussion of sex and "social equality" in *Southern History across the Color Line* (Chapel Hill: University of North Carolina Press, 2002), 112–133.

9. Rebecca Adelman, "'When I Move, You Move': Thoughts on the Fusion of Hip-Hop and Disability Activism," *Disability Studies Quarterly* 25, no. 1 (Winter 2005), www.dsq-sds.org.

10. Prince, *The Art and Science of Respect: A Memoir by James Prince*, 115.

11. As Eric Harvey recently noted, the growth of "reality rap" reflected the music's negotiation of realism and fantasy that was then evident in the early reality TV of *COPS* and *America's Most Wanted*. See Harvey, "Who Got The Camera? N.W.A.'s Embrace of 'Reality,' 1988–1992," *Pitchfork*, Mar. 31, 2015, https://pitchfork.com/thepitch/720-who-got-the-camera-nwas-embrace-of-reality-1988-1992/.

12. See, for example, Jonathan Metzl, *The Protest Psychosis: How Schizophrenia Became a Black Disease* (Boston: Beacon, 2010).

13. See Nirmala Erevelles, "Race," in *Keywords in Disability Studies*, ed. Rachel Adams, Benjamin Reiss, and David Serlin (New York: New York University Press, 2015), 145–148. There is a parallel history of institutionalization as social control for disabled people, and occasionally these two practices intersected, as in the infamous case of Junius Wilson, a deaf Black man imprisoned in a hospital for decades after being convicted of sexual assault charges from which he was ultimately exonerated. See Susan Burch and Hannah Joyner, *Unspeakable: The Story of Junius Wilson* (Chapel Hill: University of North Carolina Press, 1997).

14. For an expert discussion of the trickster's roots in the African diaspora, see Henry Louis Gates's foundational work, *The Signifying Monkey: A Theory of African-American Literary Criticism* (New York: Oxford University Press, 1989). On blues culture, see Zora Neale Hurston, "High John de Conquer," *American Mercury* (October 1943): 450–458, https://www.unz.com/print/AmMercury-1943oct-00450.

15. Mikko Koivisto, "Egresses: Countering Stereotypes of Blackness and Disability Through Horrorcore and Hip-Hop," in *Representing Communities: Discourse and Contexts*, ed. Ruth Sanz Sabido (London: Palgrave, 2017), 174.

16. Prince, *Art and Science of Respect*, 119.

17. Potts, *Geto Boys*, 58.

18. Potts, 56–57.

19. "Former Houston Officer Gets 7 Years in Killing of Woman," *New York Times*, May 2, 1990, https://www.nytimes.com/1990/05/02/us/former-houston-officer-gets-7-years-in-killing-of-woman.html.

Can't Be Stopped

1. Ed Koch, "A Call for Private Censorship," *Herald-News* (Passaic, NJ), syndicated from the *New York Post*, Sept. 14, 1990, 8.

2. Jon Pareles, "Geffen Records Pulls Plug on New Rap Album," *Santa Cruz [CA] Sentinel*, syndicated from the *New York Times*, Aug. 29, 1990, 21.

3. Koch, "A Call for Private Censorship."

4. "Rap-a-Lot Founder J. Prince Remembers Bushwick Bill."

5. Pareles, "Geffen Records Pulls Plug."

6. Tricia Rose, *The Hip Hop Wars: What We Talk About When We Talk Hip Hop—And Why It Matters* (New York: Civitas, 2008).

7. Garland-Thomson, *Extraordinary Bodies*, 6.

8. Steve Terrell, "Terrell's Tune-Up," *Santa Fe New Mexican*, Nov. 30, 1990, 65.

9. For an excellent summary of this history from the perspective of the contemporary moment (and movement), see Vilissa Thompson, "The Overlooked History of Black Disabled People," *Rewire News*, Mar. 16, 2018, https://rewire.news/article/2018/03/16/overlooked-history-black-disabled-people.

10. Jon Pareles, "Distributor Withdraws Rap Album Over Lyrics," *New York Times*, Aug. 28, 1990, https://www.nytimes.com/1990/08/28/arts/distributor-withdraws-rap-album-over-lyrics.html.

11. Pareles, "Distributor Withdraws Rap Album over Lyrics."

12. Pareles, "Geffen Records Pulls Plug on New Rap Album."

13. Bushwick Bill interview, "HoustonSoReal," http://houstonsoreal.blogspot.com/2005/01/bushwick-bill-ends-trilogy-geto-boys.html.

14. "Geto Boys Join 'Bad-Rap' Parade," *Wisconsin State Journal*, syndicated from the Associated Press, Aug. 31, 1990, D4.

15. Sara Rimer, "Obscenity or Art? Trial on Rap Lyrics Opens," *New York Times*, Oct. 17, 1990, https://www.nytimes.com/1990/10/17/us/obscenity-or-art-trial-on-rap-lyrics-opens.html.

16. Brett Koshkin, "How Tipper Gore Helped the Geto Boys Popularize Southern Rap," *Village Voice*, June 28, 2013, https://www.villagevoice.com/2013/06/28/how-tipper-gore-helped-the-geto-boys-popularize-southern-rap/.

17. "Geto Boys Join 'Bad-Rap' Parade."

18. Pareles, "Geffen Records Pulls Plug on New Rap Album."

19. Adler and Bennett, from "Geto Boys Join 'Bad-Rap' Parade"; quote from Geto Boys in Pareles, "Geffen Records Pulls Plug on New Rap Album."

20. Prince, *The Art and Science of Respect*, 119.

21. They were condemned that year at a panel at the industry's influential New Music Seminar for their counter-revolutionary content, an incident that Scarface later blamed on anti-southern bias. See Potts, *Geto Boys*, 65.

22. Frank Owen, "Censorship Isn't Def American," *Spin* (November 1990): 44.

23. Potts, *Geto Boys*, 64.

24. Greg Kot, "Rock Turns Mean and Ugly," *Chicago Tribune*, Nov. 18, 1990, sec. 13, 5.

25. Jimmy Magahern, "A Much Livelier Crew," *San Francisco Examiner*, Dec. 23, 1990, 47.

26. "2 Live Crew Part II? Houston Geto Boys Make No Apology," *Herald-News* (Passaic, NJ), Oct. 22, 1990, 2.

27. For more on the Geffen decision and its aftermath, see Potts, *Geto Boys*, 61–64; and Dan Charnas, *The Big Payback: The History of the Business of Hip-Hop* (New York: Berkley, 2011), 360–363.

28. "*Grip It! On That Other Level*" review, *The Source* (August 1990), https://ifihavent.files.wordpress.com/2007/10/getoboys_source790.jpg.

29. Charnas, *The Big Payback*, 361–362.

30. Charnas (362) notes that, in contrast, Dr. Dre's response "offered no political pretense."

31. Greil Marcus, "Notes on the Life and Death and Incandescent Banality of Rock 'n' Roll," *Esquire* (August 1992), https://greilmarcus.net/2015/04/10/notes-on-the-life-death-and-incandescent-banality-of-rock-n-roll-0892/comment-page-1/.

32. "Rap Music Blamed in Slaying of Kansas Man by 2 Youths," *Detroit Free Press*, syndicated from UPI, July 24, 1991, A4.

33. Prince, *The Art and Science of Respect*, 138.

34. Of course, there was not actually a draft for the Gulf War.

35. See John M. Kinder, *Paying with Their Bodies: American War and the Problem of the Disabled Veteran* (Chicago: University of Chicago Press, 2015).

36. Bill also claimed he'd wipe Iraq off the map with one missile rather than negotiate, a brash promise he framed as a sly slam on the white-led US military, who are not only racist hypocrites but also not serious about the mechanics of actual war-making. It's unsettling but on message.

37. William Van Deburg, *Hoodlums: Black Villains and Social Bandits in American Life* (Chicago: University of Chicago Press, 2013); Tricia Rose, *Black Noise: Rap Music and Black Culture in Contemporary America* (Boston: Wesleyan University Press, 1994).

38. Rose, *Hip Hop Wars*, 110.

39. The worst examples of Bill's homophobia come from a 2005 interview with the blog "HoustonSoReal" in which he uses multiple slurs in a sustained

attack, even suggesting that the reason why Geffen pulled the plug on their 1990 album was because he didn't like how Bill talked about gay men in "Size Ain't Shit." See Bushwick Bill interview, "HoustonSoReal."

40. Rose, *Black Noise*.

41. Stefanie Asin, "Rap Star's Remarks Anger Conventioneers," *Akron [OH] Beacon Journal*, syndicated from the *Houston Chronicle*, July 22, 1993, 7.

42. Ellen Goodman, "Time to Tear Open Envelope for Annual Equal Rites Awards," *Daily Journal* (Franklin, IN), Aug. 23, 1993, 4.

43. "Pint-Sized," in Linda Stasi (with A. J. Bentley and Michael Lewittes), "Hot Copy," *New York Daily News*, July 26, 1993, 11; "One-Eyed Midget Rapper," in Leiby, "For Four Days, White 'Ain't Right,'" *Palm Beach Post*, Oct. 3, 1993, F1, F5.

44. Rosalind Bentley, "Rappers Alienating their Allies," *Rocky Mountain News*, Aug. 2, 1993, A33; Donna Britt, "Rappers Sing Old Song of Self-Contempt," *The Press of Atlantic City*, Dec. 3, 1993, A19.

45. Kot, "Rock Turns Mean and Ugly," 5.

46. John Leland, "The Rap Attack," *Newsday*, Nov. 24, 1990.

47. Bill Wyman, "An Eye for a Truth: Bushwick Bill in Extremis," *Chicago Reader*, Sept. 24, 1992, https://www.chicagoreader.com/chicago/an-eye-for-a-truth-bushwick-bill-in-extremisturn-down-that-damn-music/Content?oid=880510; Robert Christgau, "Consumer Guide Review: *Little Big Man*," *Village Voice*, 1992, robertchristgau.com.

48. Kevin L. Carter, "Speaking Out about Rap Music's Crude Side," *Philadelphia Inquirer*, Oct. 3, 1993, F1, F10.

49. Charnas, *The Big Payback*, 418.

50. US House of Representatives, Committee on Energy and Commerce, *Music Lyrics and Commerce: Hearings Before the Subcommittee on Commerce, Consumer Protection, and Competitiveness of the Committee on Energy and Commerce*, 103rd Congress, 2nd session, Feb. 11 and May 5, 1994, https://archive.org/stream/musiclyricscomme00unit/musiclyricscomme00unit_djvu.txt.

51. US Senate, Committee on the Judiciary, *Shaping our Responses to Violent and Demeaning Imagery in Popular Music: Hearing Before the Subcommittee on Juvenile Justice of the Committee on the Judiciary*, 103rd Congress, 2nd session, Feb. 23, 1994, https://archive.org/details/shapingourrespon00unit/mode/2up.

52. Charnas, *The Big Payback*, 418.

53. James Prince notes in his memoir, *The Art and Science of Respect*, that Rap-a-Lot's attempt to sign a distribution deal was held up by Warner's board of directors because of the controversy over Ice-T and "Cop Killer."

54. Chuck Phillips, "Takin' the Rap," *Los Angeles Times*, June 9, 1995, D1, D4.

55. Phillips, D1.

56. In a June speech for the Reverend Jesse Jackson's Rainbow Coalition, Clinton cited Souljah's remarks after the LA riots in which she observed that law enforcement responded differently to the violence against white people. She rhetorically asked, "If black people kill black people every day, why not have a week and kill white people?" Clinton called this reverse racism.

57. Bernard Weinraub, "Films and Recordings Threaten Nation's Character, Dole Says," *New York Times*, June 1, 1995, https://www.nytimes.com/1995/06/01/us/films-and-recordings-threaten-nation-s-character-dole-says.html.

58. Geto Boys video, https://www.c-span.org/video/?c4455147/user-clip-geto-boys.

59. W. Speers, "Newsmakers," *Philadelphia Inquirer*, June 29, 1995, 74.

60. Steve Hochman, "At the Center of the Dole Firestorm," *Los Angeles Times*, 8.

61. The W and Mason Storm, interview with Bushwick Bill.

62. Anthony DeCurtis, "Bushwick Bill: *Phantom of the Rapra*," *Vibe* (August 1995): 136.

63. In early 1964, Malcolm X gave a speech entitled "The Ballot or the Bullet," in which he suggested the two options through which Black people could gain their freedom in the United States.

64. Vik, "Bushwick Bill and the Geto Boys: A Nightmare of Depravity," "Biochemical Slang," May 16, 2006, http://biochemicalslang.blogspot.com/2006/05/bushwick-bill-and-geto-boys-nightmare.html.

65. "Gang Founder, Serving Time, Urges Album Listeners to Vote," *News Journal* (Wilmington, DE), syndicated from the *Washington Post*, Apr. 14, 1996, 51.

66. Greg Kot, "Play On," *Chicago Tribune*, Apr. 5, 1996, A7.

67. Tracii McGregor, "Geto Life," *Vibe* 4, no. 4 (May 1996): 73.

"He Ain't What You Expect"

1. In another version of the story, told by Bill to *Vice* in 2016, his mother shot him as part of a PCP-fueled plan to get life insurance money to pay her medical bills. See "Rapper Bushwick Bill Tells Us How He Lost His Eye on PCP," *Vice* (July 2016), https://www.vice.com/en_us/article/8geavp/party-legends-ep-3.

2. Brian Coleman, *Check The Technique: Liner Notes For Hip-Hop Junkies* (New York: Villard, 2007), 227.

3. Coleman, 226.

4. Brad Jordan and Benjamin Meadows Ingram, *Diary of a Madman: The Geto Boys, Life, Death, and the Roots of Southern Rap* (New York: Dey Street Books, 2015), 74.

5. Coleman, *Check the Technique*, 226.

6. Prince, *The Art and Science of Respect*, 121.

7. In his memoir, Scarface suggests that he too was uncomfortable. "I wasn't down with that shit. It was too raw. That's why I have that look on my face in the picture, like, Holy fuck! But I was a team player." See Jordan and Ingram, *Diary of a Madman*, 74.

8. Coleman, *Check the Technique*, 226.

9. He even suggested at one point that the only reason the group did it was because they thought he was going to die. Bushwick Bill interview, "HoustonSoReal."

10. Andy Langer, "Bushwick Bill: 'I'm Not Going to Allow People to Love Me for Who I'm Not,'" *Texas Monthly* podcast, June 10, 2019, https://www.texasmonthly.com/podcast/bushwick-bill-houston-hip-hop-geto-boys/.

11. This would be repeated on the group's final album, 2005's *The Foundation*. A 1992 reissue of *Grip It!* includes a different photo, another wide shot of the group. Notably, in this image, Willie D is kneeling and is thus shorter than Bill. *'Til Death Do Us Part* (1993) shows Bill in an electric chair, surrounded by his bandmates, in an inversion (or perhaps continuation?) of the story told by the cover of *We Can't Be Stopped*. *The Resurrection* (1996) features a series of empty coffins with their lids raised; none is noticeably smaller.

12. Garland-Thomson, *Extraordinary Bodies*, 58.

13. Bushwick Bill interview, "HoustonSoReal."

14. Bushwick Bill interview, "HoustonSoReal."
15. Tamara Palmer, *Country Fried Soul: Adventures in Dirty South Hip-Hop* (San Francisco: Backbeat Books, 2005), 115.
16. Prince, *The Art and Science of Respect*, 121.
17. "Rap Commercials for Malt Liquor Draw Controversy," *Newark Advocate* (Newark, OH), syndicated from the Associated Press, Nov. 21, 1991, 16.
18. Stasi, "Hot Copy."
19. Rodney Carmichael, "Stressed Out: How 'Mind Playing Tricks on Me' Gave Anxiety a Home in Hip-Hop," *NPR*, May 29, 2019, https://www.npr.org/2019/05/29/726615663/geto-boys-mind-playing-tricks-on-me-anxiety-american-anthem.
20. Anna Hinton, "'And So I Bust Back': Violence, Race, and Disability in Hip Hop," *CLA Journal* 60, no. 3: 301.
21. Charlamagne tha God, *Shook One: Anxiety Playing Tricks on Me* (New York: Atria Books, 2018), xx.
22. Carmichael, "Stressed Out."
23. Kiana Fitzgerald, "Bushwick Bill Was Impossible to Forget," *Rolling Stone*, June 10, 2019, https://www.rollingstone.com/music/music-features/bushwick-bill-geto-boys-obituary-846397/.
24. Fitzgerald, "Bushwick Bill."
25. Interestingly, the first Geto Boys album to be released after the shooting, *'Til Death Do Us Part* (1993), doesn't feature any songs that fit this pattern, even as Bill continued his political critiques and sex-posturing. The reason is unclear, although perhaps the cover of the previous year's release of *Little Big Man* helps explain the lack of thematic overlap. The photo of Bushwick Bill in an electric chair, with his bandmates standing alongside him, suggests that Bill's seeming insanity remained a potent image for the group.
26. Mikko Koivisto, "Egresses," 175.
27. Koivisto, 175.
28. Koivisto, 176.
29. Another track, "Time Taker," features a piercing verse that Langston Collin Wilkins described as Bill "narrating his own mental struggles. It's detailed and captivating and chilling, too." Quoted in Dansby, "Geto Boys' Bushwick Bill Dies," *Houston Chronicle*, June 10, 2019.
30. Rebecca Cokley, "Little People, Big Depression," *Medium*, Sept. 12, 2017,

https://medium.com/@rebecca.cokley/little-people-big-depression-2ba274fbff68.

31. Tarbox Kiersted, "Bushwick Bill Rapped That He Had 'the Mind of a Lunatic.' Underneath, He Was Laughing," *Houston Chronicle*, June 14, 2019, https://www.houstonchronicle.com/local/gray-matters/article/Bushwick-Bill-rapped-that-he-had-the-mind-of-a-13998212.php.

Child's Play

1. W. Speers, "Newsmakers," *Philadelphia Inquirer*, June 29, 1995, 74.

2. Many horrorcore artists, including the Geto Boys, traded specifically on Black representations in horror films. For more on this tradition, see Robin R. Means Coleman, *Horror Noire: Blacks in American Horror Film from the 1890s to the Present* (New York: Routledge, 2011).

3. Neil Strauss, "Pop View: When Rap Meets the Undead," *New York Times*, Sept. 18, 1994, https://www.nytimes.com/1994/09/18/arts/pop-view-when-rap-meets-the-undead.html?sec=&spon=.

4. Roni Sarig, *Third Coast: OutKast, Timbaland and How Hip-Hop Became a Southern Thing* (New York: Da Capo, 2007), 51.

5. In her discussion of Memphis, which fostered a vibrant horrorcore scene, Zandria F. Robinson notes that the "eerie beats" and gory narratives of artists like Three 6 Mafia offered sonic representation of life in a city at the intersection of "post–Civil Rights," "postindustrial," and "post-soul" identity. See Robinson, "Soul Legacies: Hip-Hop and Historicity in Memphis," in *Hip-Hop in America: A Regional Guide*, ed. Mickey Hess (New York: Greenwood, 2009), 549. Robinson expands on horrorcore's linkage to the Black past and present in "Pioneer Up in This Bitch: Gangsta Boo and Feminist Historiographies of Rap," *New South Negress*, https://newsouthnegress.com/queenofmemphis/.

6. As Jamie Lynch notes, the artists were kindred spirits: "N-I-P, like the Geto Boys, was one of the artists pushing the limits of violent content in rap, and taking down the haters and pundits with ghastly hypothetical violence." See Lynch, "The Long, Hot Grind: How Houston Engineered an Industry of Independence," in *Hip-Hop In America: A Regional Guide*, ed. Mickey Hess (New York: Greenwood, 2009), 447.

7. David Mills, "The Geto Boys: Beating the Murder Rap," *Washington Post*,

Dec. 15, 1991, https://www.washingtonpost.com/archive/lifestyle/style/1991/12/15/the-geto-boys-beating-the-murder-rap/1f7c6694-0efb-4b9f-a288-3cc51fadfe22/.

8. Like so much of the world that Bill inhabited, this took root in the freak shows. Robert Bogdan notes, "The association of various human differences with danger, their depiction as something subhuman, animalistic and inferior, was developed as well as perpetuated by these exhibits." See Bogdan, *Freak Show: Presenting Human Oddities for Entertainment and Profit* (Chicago: University of Chicago Press, 1988), 278.

9. Chuckie was clearly modeled on Hasbro's popular "My Buddy" and "Kid Sister" toys. The two-foot-tall dolls were dressed in children's clothing and marketed as stand-ins for playmates, thus reinforcing the idea that short people are cute, cuddly, and designed to be played with.

10. Anna Hinton, "'And So I Bust Back': Violence, Race, and Disability in Hip Hop," *CLA Journal* 60, no. 3: 301.

11. Fitzgerald, "Bushwick Bill Was Impossible to Forget."

12. Lori Merish, "Cuteness and Commodity Aesthetics: Tom Thumb and Shirley Temple," in *Freakery: Cultural Spectacles of the Human Body*, ed. Rosemarie Garland-Thomson (New York: New York University Press, 1996), 190.

13. Bogdan, *Freak Show*, 4.

14. "Wonder" is from Garland-Thomson, "Introduction: From Wonder to Error — A Genealogy of Freak Discourse in Modernity," in Garland-Thomson, *Freakery*, 1–21; "Pity" is from Leslie Fiedler, *Freaks: Myths and Images of the Secret Self* (Touchstone/Simon and Schuster, 1978), 23.

15. The *Child's Play* movies were not the only ones of this era that flipped the script on the tropes of dwarf cuteness. The *Leprechaun* films, starring Warwick Davis, a dwarf, presented a murderous and lecherous version of the magical little people of Irish legend. While Bushwick Bill never referenced the Leprechaun, it's unlikely that he was unaware of the series.

16. Joan Hawkins, "'One of Us': Tod Browning's *Freaks*," in Garland-Thomson, *Freakery*, 269.

17. Garland-Thomson, *Freakery*, 269.

18. Merish, "Cuteness," 188.

19. Merish, 190.

20. Merish, 195.

21. In one shot, a "My Buddy" doll can be seen lurking in the background.
22. Langer, "Bushwick Bill."
23. Jesse Katz, "Rap Furor: New Evil or Old Story?," *Los Angeles Times*, Aug. 5, 1995, A18.
24. See Paul O'Meara, "Come Back To Hell: The Resurgence Of Memphis Horrorcore," *Hip-Hop DX*, Feb. 7, 2014, https://hiphopdx.com/editorials/id.2283/title.come-back-to-hell-the-resurgence-of-memphis-horrorcore.
25. Sarig, *Third Coast*, 275. DJ Paul has embraced his identity as a disabled rapper, including a 2019 visit to a Memphis school where he met with students in the special education program. Coleman, "Three 6 Mafia Rapper DJ Paul Reaches Out to Kids with Special Needs," televised on WREG on May 3, 2019, https://wreg.com/news/three-6-mafia-rapper-dj-paul-reaches-out-to-memphis-students/.
26. Group member Violent J. later called the Geto Boys' original the first horrorcore song. Christopher Weingarten, "Insane Clown Posse's Violent J Picks 11 Horrorcore Classics," *Spin* (October 2011), https://www.spin.com/2011/10/insane-clown-posses-violent-j-picks-11-horrorcore-classics/?page=0%2C5.
27. The group's performance of "Mind of a Lunatic" removed Bushwick Bill's verse, and the performance of "Mind Playing Tricks on Me" has Scarface rhyming the original lyrics for what became Bill's verse. For fan-shot video of the 2019 performance, see https://www.youtube.com/watch?v=D6jj06bE5cA.
28. Michael Saponara, "Eminem Pays Tribute To 'One-of-a-Kind MC' Bushwick Bill," June 12, 2019, https://www.billboard.com/articles/columns/hip-hop/8515718/eminem-tribute-bushwick-bill.
29. Bushwick Bill interview, "HoustonSoReal."

"Brand New Preacher, Rap Game Teacher"

1. Bushwick Bill interview, "HoustonSoReal," January 2001.
2. Serrano, "The H-Town Countdown, No. 16: Bushwick Bill's *Little Big Man*," *Houston Press*, Oct. 8, 2009.
3. Shaw describes being arrested eight times in two years. See Andy Langer, "Bushwick Bill: 'I'm Not Going to Allow People to Love Me for Who I'm Not,'" *Texas Monthly* podcast, June 10, 2019.

4. Bushwick Bill interview, "HoustonSoReal."

5. Ben Westhoff, "Bushwick Bill Teeters on the Brink of Deportation," *Creative Loafing*, Aug. 30, 2010, https://creativeloafing.com/content -160964-bushwick-bill-teeters-on-the-brink-of.

6. "Rap-a-Lot Founder J. Prince Remembers Bushwick Bill," *Billboard*, June 10, 2019.

7. "Murder Master Music Show," episode 618, *Blog Talk Radio*, June 26, 2019.

8. Langer, "Bushwick Bill."

9. See https://www.youtube.com/watch?v=XoMKqczpYOo.

10. Andrew Dansby, "Geto Boys' Bushwick Bill Dies," *Houston Chronicle*, June 10, 2019.

11. Westhoff, "Bushwick Bill Teeters on the Brink of Deportation."

12. "Bushwick Bill's Son Yung Knxw Speaks on the Life of the Legend | SWAY'S UNIVERSE," Dec. 11, 2019, https://www.youtube.com/watch?v =UdFkYmRVtPA.

13. Percy Crawford, "Yung Knxw, Son of Legendary Rapper, Bushwick Bill," *Hype Magazine* (May 2019), https://www.thehypemagazine.com/2019/05 /yung-knxw-son-of-legendary-rapper-bushwick-bill-i-have-no-choice -but-to-be-great-because-im-surrounded-by-greats-all-the-time/.

14. "Bushwick Bill's Son Yung Knxw."

15. Crawford, "Yung Knxw, Son of Legendary Rapper."

16. "Bushwick Bill's Son Yung Knxw."

17. He also began filming a documentary and writing a book. "Geto Boys' Bushwick Bill: I'm Fighting Stage 4 Pancreatic Cancer," TMZ, May 1, 2019, https://www.tmz.com/2019/05/01/bushwick-bill-pancreatic-cancer -stage-four-geto-boys/.

18. Some of those were recorded with Paul Wall, returning the favor for Bill's early advice. Yung KNXW later noted his gratitude to Paul for visiting Bill in the hospital during his final weeks. "Bushwick Bill's Son Yung Knxw."

19. Yung KNXW has suggested that the Geto Boys had pressured his father into going on a final tour after he announced his illness, and that Bill would have done that if the group had agreed to perform free shows to benefit cancer patients. See "Bushwick Bill's Son Yung Knxw."

20. Jordan and Ingram, "Jokester," in *Diary of a Madman*, 60.

21. Dansby, "Geto Boys' Bushwick Bill Dies."

Greatest Showmen

1. In the interest of full disclosure, I should note that my cousin appears in a small role in *The Greatest Showman*. My pride in his accomplishment and love for him does not detract from my feelings about the film.

2. For example, see Rhoda Roberts, "The Real Story behind 'The Greatest Showman' Is One of Exploitation. It's Time We Told It," *The Guardian*, July 3, 2019, https://www.theguardian.com/film/2019/jul/03/the-real -story-behind-the-greatest-showman-is-one-of-exploitation-its-time-we -told-it; and Harriet A. Washington, "Hugh Jackman's Role as P. T. Barnum Helps Erase the Showman's Violent Racism," *NBC News*, Aug. 3, 1991, https://www.nbcnews.com/think/opinion/hugh-jackman-s-role -p-t-barnum-helps-erase-showman-ncna831991.

3. Stella Young, "We're Not Here for Your Inspiration," *The Drum*, Australian Broadcasting Company, July 3, 2012, https://www.abc.net .au/news/2012-07-03/young-inspiration-porn/4107006.

4. Rebecca Cokley condemned the way that TLC's attempt to become "The Little Channel" reflects both the "average height public's obsession" with the community and their commitment to "the 'Little/Big' dichotomy" as a source of fascination. "I blame reality television for the continued exploitation of my community" in an era of continued discrimination and self-harm. See Cokley, "Little People, Big Depression," *Medium*, Sept. 12, 2017.

5. Noel Hunter, a psychologist, linked Troyer's death to the high rates of suicide among people with dwarfism and the specific factors that might lead a short-statured entertainer to experience depression. See Hunter, "Verne Troyer's Passing: What's Prejudice Got to Do with It?," http:// www.noelrhunter.com/blogs/verne_troyer/.

6. Sarah Anne Hughes, "Peter Dinklage Draws Attention to 'Dwarf Tossing' Victim Martin Henderson," *Washington Post*, Jan. 17, 2012, https://www .washingtonpost.com/blogs/celebritology/post/peter-dinklage-draws -attention-to-dwarf-tossing-victim-martin-henderson-video/2012/01/17 /gIQAL20r5P_blog.html.

7. Bogdan, *Freak Show*, 278.

8. Heffernan's reference becomes even more interesting given Three 6 Mafia

member DJ Paul's disability, which is not referenced in either the original or the Wheelchair Sports Camp track.

9. Moore chose to spell Krip-Hop Nation with a K rather than use the reappropriated term *crip* to avoid associations with the Crips, a gang that gained particular fame during the gangsta rap era. See Victoria Ann Lewis, "Crip," in *Keywords in Disability Studies*, ed. Adams, Reiss, and Serlin (New York University Press, 2015), 46.

10. Leroy F. Moore, Jr., "Krip-Hop Nation: A Soundtrack to Change," *New York Times*, July 19, 2020, https://www.nytimes.com/2020/07/19/arts/after-oscarssowhite-disability-waits-for-its-moment.html.

11. For more information, see https://kriphopnation.com/.

12. Koivisto, "Egresses," 172.

13. In 2019, Heffernan ran for mayor of Denver on a social justice platform that linked disability justice to the goals of Black Lives Matter and other social justice movements.

14. Adelman, "'When I Move, You Move.'"

15. Koivisto posits this form of resistance as an "egress" from stereotypes by Bill and other artists. See Koivisto, "Egresses," 173-177.

16. Moore, "Krip-Hop Nation."

17. Christopher Bell, "Introduction: Doing Representational Detective Work," in *Blackness and Disability: Critical Examinations and Cultural Interventions*, ed. Christopher Bell (Ann Arbor: Michigan State University Press, 2012), 4. Crucial work is now being done in this area by the Harriet Tubman Collective, a group of disabled Black organizers who focus on policing, prison abolition, and other issues. See Harriet Tubman Collective, "Disability Solidarity: Completing the 'Vision for Black Lives,'" in *Disability Visibility: First-Person Stories from the Twenty-First Century*, ed. Alice Wong (New York: Vintage, 2020), 236-242.

18. Moya Bailey, "'The Illest': Disability as Metaphor in Hip-Hop Music," in Bell, *Blackness and Disability*, 141-148.

19. Two recent anthologies have collected some of these voices along with those of honored elders. See Wong, *Disability Visibility: First-Person Stories from the Twenty-First Century* (New York: Vintage, 2020); and Caitlin Wood, *Criptiques* (n.p.: May Day Publishing, 2014).

20. Barbarin tweets at @CrutchesAndSpice; Thompson at @Vilissa

Thompson; Pulrang at @AndrewPulrang; and Wong at @SFDireWolf. Little Person advocates, including Rebecca Cokley (@RebeccaCokley) and Eugene Grant (@MrEugeneGrant), are also active, as well as many, many more.

21. Garland-Thomson, *Extraordinary Bodies*, 13.
22. Potts, *Geto Boys*, 28.

BIBLIOGRAPHY

Adelman, Rebecca. "'When I Move, You Move': Thoughts on the Fusion of Hip-Hop and Disability Activism." *Disability Studies Quarterly* 25, no. 1 (Winter 2005), https://dsq-sds.org/article/view/526/703.

Adelson, Betty. *The Lives of Dwarfs: Their Journey from Public Curiosity toward Social Liberation*. New Brunswick, NJ: Rutgers University Press, 2005.

Asin, Stefanie. "Rap Star's Remarks Anger Conventioneers." *Akron (OH) Beacon Journal*, July 22, 1993, 7, syndicated from the *Houston Chronicle*.

Associated Press. "Geto Boys Join 'Bad-Rap' Parade." *Wisconsin State Journal*, Aug. 31, 1990, D4.

———. "Rap Commercials for Malt Liquor Draw Controversy." *Newark (OH) Advocate*, Nov. 21, 1991, 16.

———. "Rapper Takes on a New Name." *Kokomo (IN) Tribune*, May 5, 1995, 6.

Bailey, Moya. "'The Illest': Disability as Metaphor in Hip-Hop Music." In *Blackness and Disability*, edited by Christopher Bell, 141–148. Ann Arbor: Michigan State University Press, 2012.

Bell, Christopher. "Introduction: Doing Representational Detective Work." In *Blackness and Disability*, edited by Christopher Bell (Ann Arbor: Michigan State University Press, 2012), 1–8.

Bentley, Rosalind. "Rappers Alienating Their Allies." *Rocky Mountain News*, Aug. 2, 1993, A33.

Billboard. "Rap-a-Lot Founder: 'He Was Almost Like a Bible Scholar.'" June 10, 2019. https://www.billboard.com/articles/columns/hip-hop/8515201/bushwick-bill-j-prince-interview.

Bogdan, Robert. *Freak Show: Presenting Human Oddities for Entertainment and Profit*. Chicago: University of Chicago Press, 1988.

Boster, Dea H. *African American Slavery and Disability: Bodies, Property and Power in the Antebellum South, 1800–1860.* New York: Routledge, 2012.

Britt, Donna. "Rappers Sing Old Song of Self-Contempt." *Press of Atlantic City (NJ),* Dec. 3, 1993, A19.

Burch, Susan, and Hannah Joyner. *Unspeakable: The Story of Junius Wilson.* Chapel Hill: University of North Carolina Press, 1997.

Bushwick Bill interview. "HoustonSoReal" (January 2005). http://houstonsoreal.blogspot.com/2005/01/bushwick-bill-ends-trilogy-geto-boys.html.

"Bushwick Bill's Son Yung Knxw Speaks on the Life of the Legend | SWAY'S UNIVERSE." YouTube, Dec. 11, 2019. https://www.youtube.com/watch?v=UdFkYmRVtPA.

Caramanica, Jon. "Bushwick Bill, Rapper Who Told Harrowing Tales in Geto Boys, Is Dead at 52." *New York Times,* June 10, 2019. https://www.nytimes.com/2019/06/10/obituaries/bushwick-bill-dead.html.

Carmichael, Rodney. "Stressed Out: How 'Mind Playing Tricks On Me' Gave Anxiety a Home in Hip-Hop." NPR, May 29, 2019, https://www.npr.org/2019/05/29/726615663/geto-boys-mind-playing-tricks-on-me-anxiety-american-anthem.

Carter, Kevin L. "Speaking Out about Rap Music's Crude Side." *Philadelphia Inquirer,* Oct. 3, 1993, F1, F10.

Cassuto, Leonard. "Freak." In *Keywords in Disability Studies,* edited by Rachel Adams, Benjamin Reiss, and David Serlin, 85–88. New York: New York University Press, 2015.

Chang, Jeff. *Can't Stop Won't Stop: A History of the Hip-Hop Generation.* New York: Picador, 2005.

Charlamagne tha God. *Shook One: Anxiety Playing Tricks On Me.* New York: Atria, 2018.

Charnas, Dan. *The Big Payback: The History of the Business of Hip-Hop.* New York: New American Library, 2011.

Chriss, Catherine. "For Houston's Geto Boys, Anything Goes in the World of Gangsta Rap." *Houston Chronicle,* Apr. 5, 1992, 10.

Christgau, Robert. "Consumer Guide Review: *Little Big Man.*" *Village Voice,* 1992. See robertchristgau.com.

Cokley, Rebecca. "Little People, Big Depression." *Medium*, Sep. 12, 2017. https://medium.com/@rebecca.cokley/little-people-big-depression -2ba274fbff68.

Coleman, Alex. "Three 6 Mafia Rapper DJ Paul Reaches Out to Kids with Special Needs." Televised on WREG on May 3, 2019. https://wreg.com /news/three-6-mafia-rapper-dj-paul-reaches-out-to-memphis -students/.

Coleman, Brian. *Check the Technique: Liner Notes for Hip-Hop Junkies*. New York: Villard, 2007.

Coleman, Robin R. Means. *Horror Noire: Blacks in American Horror Film from the 1890s to the Present*. New York: Routledge, 2011.

Crawford, Percy. "Yung Knxw, Son of Legendary Rapper, Bushwick Bill." *Hype Magazine* (May 2019). https://www.thehypemagazine.com/2019 /05/yung-knxw-son-of-legendary-rapper-bushwick-bill-i-have-no -choice-but-to-be-great-because-im-surrounded-by-greats-all-the -time/.

Dansby, Andrew. "Geto Boys' Bushwick Bill Dies." *Houston Chronicle*, June 10, 2019. https://www.houstonchronicle.com/entertainment /music/article/Geto-Boys-Bushwick-Bill-dies-13964959.php.

DeCurtis, Anthony. "Bushwick Bill: *Phantom of the Rapra*." *Vibe* (August 1995): 136.

Deburg, William Van. *Hoodlums: Black Villains and Social Bandits in American Life*. Chicago: University of Chicago Press, 2013.

Erevelles, Nirmala. "Race." In *Keywords in Disability Studies*, edited by Rachel Adams, Benjamin Reiss, and David Serlin, 145–148. New York: New York University Press, 2015.

Ewoodzie, Joseph C., Jr. *Break Beats in the Bronx: Rediscovering Hip-Hop's Early Years*. Chapel Hill: University of North Carolina Press, 2015.

Faniel, Maco. *Hip-Hop in Houston: The Origin and the Legacy*. Charleston, SC: History Press, 2013.

Fiedler, Leslie. *Freaks: Myths and Images of the Secret Self*. Touchstone/ Simon & Schuster, 1978.

Fitzgerald, Kiana. "Bushwick Bill Was Impossible to Forget." *Rolling*

Stone, June 10, 2019. https://www.rollingstone.com/music/music
-features/bushwick-bill-geto-boys-obituary-846397/.

Fricke, David. "Randy Newman: My Life in 15 Songs." *Rolling Stone*, Sep. 15, 2017. https://www.rollingstone.com/music/music-lists/randy
-newman-my-life-in-15-songs-202825/short-people-204315/.

"Gang Founder, Serving Time, Urges Album Listeners to Vote." *News Journal* (Wilmington DE), syndicated from the *Washington Post*, Apr. 14, 1996, 51.

Garland-Thomson, Rosemarie. *Extraordinary Bodies: Figuring Physical Disability in American Culture and Literature*. New York: Columbia University Press, 1997.

———. "Introduction: From Wonder to Error — A Genealogy of Freak Discourse in Modernity." In *Freakery: Cultural Spectacles of the Extraordinary Body*, edited by Garland-Thomson, 1–21. New York: New York University Press, 1996.

———. *Staring: How We Look*. New York: Oxford University Press, 2009.

Gates, Henry Louis, Jr. *The Signifying Monkey: A Theory of African-American Literary Criticism*. New York: Oxford University Press, 1989.

Gerber, David. "The 'Careers' of People Exhibited in Freak Shows: The Problem of Volition and Valorization." In *Freakery: Cultural Spectacles of the Extraordinary Body*, edited by Rosemarie Garland-Thomson, 38–55. New York: New York University Press, 1996.

Goodman, Ellen. "Time to Tear Open Envelope for Annual Equal Rites Awards." Franklin (IN) *Daily Journal*, Aug. 23, 1993, 4.

Grant, Eugene. "The Fearless Benjamin Lay: Activist, Abolitionist, Dwarf Person." In *Disability Visibility: First-Person Stories from the Twenty-First Century*, edited by Alice Wong, 229–231. New York: Vintage, 2020.

"*Grip It! On That Other Level*." Review. *The Source* (August 1990). https://ifihavent.files.wordpress.com/2007/10/getoboys_source790.jpg.

Hamilton, Isobel. "Writer and Activist Shares Twitter Thread about the Language People with Dwarfism Have to Deal With." *Mashable*, Mar. 1, 2018. https://mashable.com/2018/03/01/eugene-grant-thread-people
-dwarfism-language/.

Harriet Tubman Collective. "Disability Solidarity: Completing the 'Vision for Black Lives.' In *Disability Visibility: Stories from the Twenty-First Century*, edited by Alice Wong, 236–242. New York: Vintage, 2020.

Harvey, Eric. "Who Got The Camera? N.W.A.'s Embrace of 'Reality,' 1988–1992." *Pitchfork*, Mar. 31, 2015. https://pitchfork.com/thepitch/720-who-got-the-camera-nwas-embrace-of-reality-1988-1992/.

Hawkins, Joan. "'One of Us': Tod Browning's *Freaks*." In *Freakery: Cultural Spectacles of the Human Body*, edited by Rosemarie Garland-Thomson, 265–276. New York: New York University Press, 1996.

Herald-News (Passaic, NJ). "2 Live Crew Part II? Houston Geto Boys Make No Apology." Oct. 22, 1990, 2.

Hinton, Anna. "'And So I Bust Back': Violence, Race, and Disability in Hip Hop." *CLA Journal* 60, no. 3: 290–304.

Hochman, Steve, "At the Center of the Dole Firestorm." *Los Angeles Times*, July 30, 1995, 6–9, 82–83.

Hughes, Sarah Anne. "Peter Dinklage Draws Attention to 'Dwarf Tossing' Victim, Martin Henderson." *Washington Post*, Jan. 17, 2012. https://www.washingtonpost.com/blogs/celebritology/post/peter-dinklage-draws-attention-to-dwarf-tossing-victim-martin-henderson-video/2012/01/17/gIQAL20r5P_blog.html.

Hunter, Noel R. "Verne Troyer's Passing: What's Prejudice Got To Do With It?" http://www.noelrhunter.com/blogs/verne_troyer/.

Hurston, Zora Neale. "High John de Conquer." *American Mercury* (October 1943): 450–458. https://www.unz.com/print/AmMercury-1943oct-00450.

Johnson, Walter. *Soul By Soul: Life Inside the Antebellum Slave Market*. Cambridge, MA: Harvard University Press, 1999.

Jordan, Brad, and Benjamin Meadows Ingram. *Diary of a Madman: The Geto Boys, Life, Death, and the Roots of Southern Rap*. New York: Dey Street Books, 2015.

Katz, Jesse. "Rap Furor: New Evil or Old Story?" *Los Angeles Times*, Aug. 5, 1995, A1, A18–19.

Kenney, Shawna. "Geto Boy: An Interview with Bushwick Bill." *Pitchfork*, Sep. 8, 2015. https://pitchfork.com/thepitch/893-geto-boy-an-interview-with-bushwick-bill/.

Kiersted, Tarbox. "Bushwick Bill Rapped That He Had 'the Mind of a Lunatic.' Underneath, He Was Laughing." *Houston Chronicle*, June 14, 2019. https://www.houstonchronicle.com/local/gray-matters/article/Bushwick-Bill-rapped-that-he-had-the-mind-of-a-13998212.php.

Kinder, John M. *Paying with Their Bodies: American War and the Problem of the Disabled Veteran*. Chicago: University of Chicago Press, 2015.

Koch, Ed. "A Call for Private Censorship." *Herald-News* (Passaic, NJ), syndicated from the *New York Post*, Sep. 14, 1990, 8.

Koivisto, Mikko. "Egresses: Countering Stereotypes of Blackness and Disability Through Horrorcore and Hip-Hop." In *Representing Communities: Discourse and Contexts*, edited by Ruth Sanz Sabido, 163–180. London: Palgrave, 2017.

Koshkin, Brett. "How Tipper Gore Helped the Geto Boys Popularize Southern Rap." *Village Voice*, June 23, 2013. https://www.villagevoice.com/2013/06/28/how-tipper-gore-helped-the-geto-boys-popularize-southern-rap/.

Kot, Greg. "Play On." *Chicago Tribune*, Apr. 5, 1996, A7.

———. "Rock Turns Mean and Ugly." *Chicago Tribune*, Nov. 18, 1990, sec. 13, 4–5, 17.

Langer, Andy. "Bushwick Bill: 'I'm Not Going to Allow People to Love Me for Who I'm Not.'" *Texas Monthly* podcast, June 10, 2019. https://www.texasmonthly.com/podcastbushwick-bill-houston-hip-hop-geto-boys/.

Leiby, Richard. "For Four Days, White 'Ain't Right.'" *Palm Beach Post*, Oct. 3, 1993, F1, F5.

Leland, John. "The Rap Attack." *Newsday*, Nov. 24, 1990.

Lewis, Victoria Ann. "Crip." In *Keywords in Disability Studies*, edited by Rachel Adams, Benjamin Reiss, and David Serlin, 46–48. New York: New York University Press, 2015.

Little People of America. "LPA Issues Statement to Abolish the 'M' Word." LPA online, September 2015. https://www.lpaonline.org/the-m-word.

Lomax, John Nova. "The Geto Boys and Public Enemy, 25 Years Ago." *Houstonia*, Aug. 28, 2013. https://www.houstoniamag.com/arts-and

-culture/2013/08/the-geto-boys-and-public-enemy-together-august
-2013.

Lott, Eric. *Love and Theft: Blackface Minstrelsy and the American Working Class*. New York: Oxford University Press, 1995.

Lynch, Jamie. "The Long, Hot Grind: How Houston Engineered an Industry of Independence." In *Hip-Hop in America: A Regional Guide*, edited by Mickey Hess, 429–465. New York: Greenwood, 2009.

Magahern, Jimmy. "A Much Livelier Crew." *San Francisco Examiner*, Dec. 23, 1990, 47–48.

Marcus, Greil. "Notes on the Life and Death and Incandescent Banality of Rock 'n' Roll." *Esquire* (August 1992). https://greilmarcus.net/2015/04 /10/notes-on-the-life-death-and-incandescent-banality-of-rock-n-roll -0892/comment-page-1/.

McGregor, Tracii. "Geto Life." *Vibe* 4, no. 4 (May 1996): 72–76.

McKay, George. *Shakin' All Over: Popular Music and Disability*. Ann Arbor: University of Michigan Press, 2013.

Merish, Lori. "Cuteness and Commodity Aesthetics: Tom Thumb and Shirley Temple." In *Freakery: Cultural Spectacles of the Human Body*, edited by Rosemarie Garland-Thomson, 185–203. New York: New York University Press, 1996.

Metzl, Jonathan. *The Protest Psychosis: How Schizophrenia Became a Black Disease*. Boston: Beacon, 2010.

Mills, David. "The Geto Boys: Beating the Murder Rap." *Washington Post*, Dec. 15, 1991. https://www.washingtonpost.com/archive/lifestyle /style/1991/12/15/the-geto-boys-beating-the-murder-rap/1f7c6694 -0efb-4b9f-a288-3cc51fadfe22/.

Moore, Leroy F., Jr. "Krip-Hop Nation: A Soundtrack to Change." *New York Times*, July 19, 2020. https://www.nytimes.com/2020/07/19/arts /after-oscarssowhite-disability-waits-for-its-moment.html.

"Murder Master Music Show." Episode 618. Blog Talk Radio, June 26, 2019. https://www.blogtalkradio.com/murdermastermusicshow/2019/07/26 /episode-618-yung-knxw/.

Owen, Frank. "Censorship Isn't Def American." *Spin* (November 1990): 43–46.

Painter, Nell Irvin. *Southern History Across the Color Line*. Chapel Hill: University of North Carolina Press, 2002.

Palmer, Tamara. *Country Fried Soul: Adventures in Dirty South Hip-Hop*. San Francisco: Backbeat Books, 2005.

Pareles, Jon. "Distributor Withdraws Rap Album over Lyrics." *New York Times*, Aug. 28, 1990. https://www.nytimes.com/1990/08/28/arts/distributor-withdraws-rap-album-over-lyrics.html.

———. "Geffen Records Pulls Plug on New Rap Album." *Santa Cruz (CA) Sentinel*, syndicated from the *New York Times*, Aug. 29, 1990, 21.

Phillips, Chuck. "Takin' the Rap." *Los Angeles Times*, June 9, 1995, D1, D4.

Potts, Rolf. *The Geto Boys*. New York: Continuum, 2016.

Powell, Joanna. "Randy Newman's 'Short People.'" *Entertainment Weekly*, Dec. 11, 1992. https://ew.com/article/1992/12/11/randy-newmans-short-people/.

Prince, James, with Jasmine D. Waters. *The Art and Science of Respect: A Memoir by James Prince*. N-The-Water, 2018.

Reiss, Benjamin. "P. T. Barnum, Joice Heth, and Antebellum Spectacles of Race." *American Quarterly* 51, no. 1 (March 1999): 78–107.

———. *The Showman and the Slave: Race, Death, and Memory in Barnum's America*. Cambridge, MA: Harvard University Press, 2010.

Relic, Peter. "The Return." *XXL Magazine* (January/February 2005). Reprinted in *Da Capo Best Music Writing 2006*, edited by Mary Gaitskill and Daphne Carr, 231–239. Cambridge, MA: Da Capo, 2006.

Rimer, Sara. "Obscenity or Art? Trial on Rap Lyrics Opens." *New York Times*, Oct. 17, 1990. https://www.nytimes.com/1990/10/17/us/obscenity-or-art-trial-on-rap-lyrics-opens.html.

Roberts, Rhoda. "The Real Story behind 'The Greatest Showman' Is One of Exploitation. It's Time We Told It." *The Guardian*, July 3, 2019. https://www.theguardian.com/film/2019/jul/03/the-real-story-behind-the-greatest-showman-is-one-of-exploitation-its-time-we-told-it.

Robinson, Zandria F. "Pioneer Up in This Bitch: Gangsta Boo and Feminist Historiographies of Rap." *New South Negress* (n.d.). https://newsouthnegress.com/queenofmemphis/.

———. "Soul Legacies: Hip-Hop and Historicity in Memphis." In *Hip-Hop in America: A Regional Guide*, edited by Mickey Hess, 549–576. New York: Greenwood, 2009.

Rose, Tricia. *Black Noise: Rap Music and Black Culture in Contemporary America*. Boston: Wesleyan University Press, 1994. Kindle edition.
———. *The Hip Hop Wars: What We Talk About When We Talk Hip Hop—And Why It Matters*. New York: Civitas, 2008.

Rowden, Terry. *The Songs of Blind Folk: African American Musicians and the Cultures of Blindness*. Ann Arbor: University of Michigan Press, 2009.

Saponara, Michael. "Eminem Pays Tribute to 'One-of-a-Kind MC' Bushwick Bill." *Billboard*, June 12, 2019. https://www.billboard.com /articles/columns/hip-hop/8515718/eminem-tribute-bushwick-bill.

Sarig, Roni. *Third Coast: OutKast, Timbaland, and How Hip-Hop Became a Southern Thing*. New York: Da Capo, 2007.

Serrano, Shea. "The H-Town Countdown, No. 16: Bushwick Bill's *Little Big Man*." *Houston Press*, Oct. 8, 2009. https://www.houstonpress .com/music/the-h-town-countdown-no-16-bushwick-bills-little-big -man-6529491.

Setaro, Shawn. "Bushwick Bill Can't Be Stopped." *Complex*, June 10, 2019. https://www.complex.com/music/2019/06/bushwick-bill-obituary.

Speers, W. "Newsmakers." *Philadelphia Inquirer*, June 29, 1995, 74.

Stasi, Linda, with A. J. Bentley and Michael Lewittes. "Hot Copy." *New York Daily News*, July 26, 1993, 11.

Steptoe, Tyina L. *Houston Bound: Culture and Color in a Jim Crow City*. Berkeley: University of California Press, 2016.

Stras, Laurie. "Sing a Song of Difference: Connie Boswell and a Discourse of Disability in Jazz." *Popular Music* 28, no. 3 (October 2009): 297–322.
———. "'Who Told You That Lie?': Picturing Connie Boswell." In *Reframing Representations of Women: Figuring, Fashioning, Portraiting, and Telling in the "Picturing" Women Project*, edited by Susan Shifrin, 251–267. London: Ashgate, 2008.

Straus, Joseph N. *Extraordinary Measures: Disability in Music*. New York: Oxford University Press, 2011. eBook.

Bibliography

Strauss, Neil. "Pop View: When Rap Meets the Undead." *New York Times*, Sep. 18, 1994. https://www.nytimes.com/1994/09/18/arts/pop-view-when-rap-meets-the-undead.html?sec=&spon=

Terrell, Steve. "Terrell's Tune-Up." *Santa Fe New Mexican*, Nov. 30, 1990, 65.

Thompson, Vilissa. "The Overlooked History of Black Disabled People." *Rewire News*, Mar. 16, 2018. https://rewire.news/article/2018/03/16/overlooked-history-black-disabled-people.

TMZ. "Geto Boys' Bushwick Bill: I'm Fighting Stage 4 Pancreatic Cancer." May 1, 2019. https://www.tmz.com/2019/05/01/bushwick-bill-pancreatic-cancer-stage-four-geto-boys/.

Understanding Dwarfism Program. "What Is the Correct Terminology?" http://www.udprogram.com/correct-terminology.

UPI. "Rap Music Blamed in Slaying of Kansas Man by 2 Youths." *Detroit Free Press*, July 24, 1991, A4.

US House of Representatives, Committee on Energy and Commerce. *Music Lyrics and Commerce : Hearings Before the Subcommittee on Commerce, Consumer Protection, and Competitiveness of the Committee on Energy and Commerce, House of Representatives*, 103rd Congress, 2nd session, Feb. 11 and May 5, 1994. https://archive.org/stream/musiclyricscomme00unit/musiclyricscomme00unit_djvu.txt.

US Senate, Committee of the Judiciary. *Shaping Our Responses to Violent and Demeaning Imagery in Popular Music: Hearing Before the Subcommittee on Juvenile Justice of the Committee on the Judiciary*. 103rd Congress, 2nd session, February 23, 1994. https://archive.org/details/shapingourrespon00unit/mode/2u.

Vice. "Rapper Bushwick Bill Tells Us How He Lost His Eye on PCP." July 21, 2016. https://www.vice.com/en_us/article/8geavp/party-legends-ep-3.

Vik. "Bushwick Bill and the Geto Boys: A Nightmare of Depravity." "Biochemical Slang," May 16, 2006. http://biochemicalslang.blogspot.com/2006/05/bushwick-bill-and-geto-boys-nightmare.html.

The W and Mason Storm. Interview with Bushwick Bill. The 411 Online, July 7, 1995. http://www.the411online.com/bill.html.

Bibliography

Walker, Lance Scott. *Houston Rap Tapes: An Oral History of Bayou City Hip-Hop.* Austin: University of Texas Press, 2018.

Washington, Harriet A. "Hugh Jackman's Role as P. T. Barnum Helps Erase the Showman's Violent Racism." NBC News, Aug. 3, 1991. https://www.nbcnews.com/think/opinion/hugh-jackman-s-role-p-t-barnum-helps-erase-showman-ncna831991.

Weingarten, Christopher. "Insane Clown Posse's Violent J Picks 11 Horrorcore Classics." *Spin* (October 2011). https://www.spin.com/2011/10/insane-clown-posses-violent-j-picks-11-horrorcore-classics/?page=0%2C5.

Weinraub, Bernard. "Films and Recordings Threaten Nation's Character, Dole Says." *New York Times*, June 1, 1995. https://www.nytimes.com/1995/06/01/us/films-and-recordings-threaten-nation-s-character-dole-says.html.

Westhoff, Ben. "Bushwick Bill Teeters on the Brink of Deportation." *Creative Loafing*, Aug. 30, 2010. https://creativeloafing.com/content-160964-bushwick-bill-teeters-on-the-brink-of.

Wong, Alice, ed. *Disability Visibility: First-Person Stories from the Twenty-First Century.* New York: Vintage, 2020.

Wood, Caitlin, ed. *Criptiques.* N.p.: May Day Publishing, 2014.

Wyman, Bill. "Turn Down That Damn Music!: An Eye for a Truth: Bushwick Bill in Extremis." *Chicago Reader*, Sep. 24, 1992. https://www.chicagoreader.com/chicago/an-eye-for-a-truth-bushwick-bill-in-extremisturn-down-that-damn-music/Content?oid=880510.

Young, Stella. "We're Not Here for Your Inspiration." *The Drum*, July 3, 2012. https://www.abc.net.au/news/2012-07-03/young-inspiration-porn/4107006.